Client/Server
System Design
and Implementation

Other Books in the McGraw-Hill Series on Computer Communications

Client/Server
System Design
and Implementation

Larry T. Vaughn

McGraw-Hill, Inc.

New York San Francisco Washington, D.C. Auckland Bogotá
Caracas Lisbon London Madrid Mexico City Milan
Montreal New Delhi San Juan Singapore
Sydney Tokyo Toronto

Library of Congress Cataloging-in-Publication Data

Vaughn, Larry T.
    Client/server system design and implementation / Larry T. Vaughn.
        p.   cm — (McGraw-Hill series on computer communications)
    Includes index.
    ISBN 0-07-067375-6
    1. Client/server computing.   2. System design.   I. Title.
II. Series.
QA76.9.C55V38   1994
004'.36—dc20   94-1539
                                                                       CIP

1 2 3 4 5 6 7 8 9 0   DOC/DOC   9 0 9 8 7 6 5 4

ISBN 0-07-067375-6

*The sponsoring editor for this book was Jerry Papke, the editing super-
visor was Paul R. Sobel, and the production supervisor was Pamela A.
Pelton. It was set in Century Schoolbook by McGraw-Hill's Professional
Book Group composition unit.*

Printed and bound by R. R. Donnelley & Sons Company.

 This book is printed on recycled, acid-free paper containing a
minimum of 50% recycled de-inked fiber.

To Mickey, without whose encouragement this book would never have been completed

Contents

Part 3. Building Client/Server Applications

Preface

Every industry and technical discipline has its own vocabulary. Although characterized by many as *techno-babble*, such technical vocabulary serves a valuable purpose in that it is often needed to introduce and describe truly new concepts. Relatively immature, rapidly evolving, and technology driven, the information processing industry's technical vocabulary has grown at an exponential rate. Unfortunately, much of this growth has come from hardware and software vendors seeking to gain competitive market advantage for their newest whiz-bang technology, industry publications seeking to boost their circulation, or technology analysts wishing to be the first to identify the latest breakthrough.

As a consultant, I should welcome this veritable blizzard of techno-babble. After all, the more confused the consumers of this technology are, the greater the need for so-called experts to sort the wheat from the chaff. But as a developer seeking to deliver system solutions I find that the "noise" ratio of hype to truth is becoming a serious obstacle in identifying truly innovative technologies that can be applied to real-world problems. Batch processing, database management, centralized processing, client/server processing, data modeling, distributed processing, hierarchical databases, local area networks, mainframe, minicomputer, multiprocessing, multithreading, multiuser, object orientation, peer-to-peer, personal computer, relational databases, server, structured analysis, transaction processing, virtual memory, wide-area networks, workstation, etc. What are these things? Which represent truly significant new solutions and tools, which represent the latest market hype, and which are just technologies looking for a problem to solve?

This book was written for the information systems professionals who are tasked with providing highly functional and cost-effective system solutions in support of their organization's business solutions and who are contemplating or are already in the process of delivering those solutions through client/server technologies. It provides both context and detail to address the needs of the following:

- The information systems executives tasked with integrating information systems into the basic fabric of the enterprise's operations and strategy and who need to understand the basic technological foundations, benefits, and obstacles that must be overcome before this new technology can be deployed effectively.

- The systems development line managers who have to face the move to the more open, flexible, and less stable client/server environments while continuing to support legacy systems based on closed proprietary development platforms.

- The project leaders tasked with installing the technological infrastructure, choosing the appropriate tools, and developing new systems structured and designed specifically to take advantage of the strengths of client/server technologies.

- The developers seeking to deepen their understanding of the new and totally alien environment within which they will be designing and building system solutions.

This book is divided into three parts. Part 1 provides a definition of client/server architecture, outlines the basic differences between this architectural approach and the traditional centralized mainframe-centric architecture, and discusses the impact this change can make to your enterprise. It identifies the specific benefits that are promised by the architecture and, more importantly, discusses the obstacles that must be surmounted and pitfalls to be avoided before these benefits can be realized.

Part 2 identifies and explains the technologies used by the client/server architecture. It breaks these technologies down into client, network, and server components and discusses how these technologies interact to provide a cost-effective, high-performance and stable foundation for delivering business system solutions to the enterprise. It discusses how these changes impact the application developer attempting the transition from the traditional mainframe environment and provides guidelines and suggestions for selecting appropriate technologies to establish a stable foundation.

Part 3 offers a perspective that can help you decide if migrating to a client/server architecture is right for your enterprise and provides the framework for planning, preparing, and executing a strategy to develop and deliver client/server system solutions to your enterprise. It discusses planning and preparation and the activities necessary to establish an infrastructure within which development can take place. It identifies tools and techniques that have proven useful to capture business needs and develop applications that meet those needs. Finally, it proposes a new approach to application development that incorporates modern concepts and principles that are emerging from the research and experiments being conducted and nurtured by such organizations as the American Society for Manufacturing Excellence, the American Society for Quality Control, the American Institute of Research, and the American Quality Foundation, and implemented and proven by forward thinking enterprises throughout the industrial segments of our economy.

As an information processing professional over the past 18 years, I have studied, worked with, fought against, fought for, and tried to apply practically every new whiz-bang to come down the pike, and I have come to the conclusion that there are very few that represent truly significant advances in the way system solutions are developed and delivered. The impact of these few has been dramatic, each representing a significant and profound change in the way developers approach problems and deliver solutions. I believe the client/server approach to application design to be such a development, as significant in its impact as the shift from batch processing to transaction processing, tape data storage to multi-user databases, and the introduction of the personal computer.

But what is client/server processing? Where does it fit in today's environment? How is it different from current practice? How is it the same? What impact will it have on your organization? My goal in writing this book is to answer these questions and hopefully arm the information systems professional, technical managers, and MIS executives with the basic knowledge needed to apply this approach to real-world problems in their organizations. Do not be misled by the objective and frank discussion of the good, the bad, and the ugly aspects of the client/server approach. I am an unabashed promoter of the client/server approach and believe it represents a genuine paradigm shift in the development of computer applications, and as a fellow information systems professional, I hope that you find this book to be a useful tool in your own application of this approach.

Acknowledgments

It is essential to remember that all successful systems development projects are a collaborative effort of individuals with varying backgrounds and skills who come together as a team to focus on a specific objective and come away from the process with greater personal and professional understanding. Ultimately, the only unsuccessful development effort is the one from which nothing is learned.

To celebrate one such special team I'd like to take this opportunity to acknowledge the contributions of Peter Thawley, Annette Runckel, Dave Webb, Katharine Hanson, and Bruce Randall to the experience which made this book possible.

Larry T. Vaughn

Introduction

1

Client/Server Architecture

What is "client/server architecture"? Webster states that architecture is "the art and science of designing and erecting a building." Within the context of information systems we could then say that client/server architecture must be an approach to the design of an information system. As a general definition, this is fine as far as it goes but fails to describe the approach and what differentiates it from other approaches. There appears to be general agreement that client/server architecture is an approach to the design of a software application that decomposes the application into a small number of server functions that provide commonly used services and a larger number of client functions that perform more narrowly defined work in reliance on the common services provided by the server functions. Even this more descriptive definition does not go far enough to fully encompass the complex nature of the approach. Almost implicit in the approach is the assumption that the server and client functions of the resulting application will be executing on different interconnected hardware platforms. An expanded and more fully descriptive definition would therefore be

> Client/server architecture is an application design approach that results in the decomposition of an information system into a small number of server functions, executing on one or more hardware platforms, that provide commonly used services to a larger number of client functions, executing on one or more different

3

but interconnected hardware platforms, that perform more narrowly defined work in reliance on the common services provided by the server functions.

Even with a full definition and despite the large numbers of articles and seminars on this subject, there is still confusion in many information system professionals' minds regarding the application of this approach and its impact in organizations using more traditional architectures. Like art, where few can agree on a definition but everyone knows it when they see it, "client/server architecture" means different things to different people depending on their perceptions and backgrounds. Because of this any meaningful discussion of client/server architecture should begin with a review of the other architectural approaches most commonly used.

Centralized Multiuser Architecture

An architectural approach that designs an application so that all functional and data components of the application reside and execute upon one centralized computing platform (Fig. 1.1) used by multiple simultaneous users of that application. Examples of applications using this approach include order entry, accounting, manufacturing control, automated teller machines, and reservation systems.

This approach is the most common architecture used for business applications based on mainframe and minicomputer technologies, and its use is driven by a number of factors, the most important of which are

- The need to leverage the costly investment in hardware, software, and technical support staff represented by these cen-

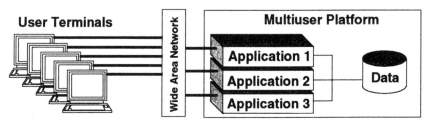

Figure 1.1   Centralized multiuser architecture.

tralized computers across as many applications and users as possible.

- The need to provide large numbers of simultaneous users (200 to 10,000+) with reliable and stable access to one or more special-purpose applications.
- The need to provide centralized storage for very large databases shared by many simultaneous users.
- The need to minimize the amount of data that flows across relatively slow (9.6 kbits/s to 1.5 Mbits/s) and expensive wide area networks.

Strengths

- This technology tends to be very stable, reliable, and well supported by responsible original equipment manufacturers (OEMs).
- It is capable of providing cost-effective application functionality and shared data access to thousands of users.
- A single OEM vendor can often provide all the system-level hardware, software, and networking components. This "one-stop shopping" capability significantly simplifies the administration and management of the environment.
- There is a large pool of highly skilled technical staff who are available to provide technical, operational, and developmental support.
- Business application software is commercially available from the OEMs and third-party vendors across a wide range of categories.

Weaknesses

- Technologies are proprietary and, with a few exceptions, generally incompatible across OEM vendors. In some cases this incompatibility even extends to different model lines from the same vendor.
- Technology within this category is expensive to acquire. Implementation costs can also be substantial as these platforms often require controlled environments with raised flooring, massive air- and liquid-cooling plants, sophisticated

power distribution, and special-purpose fire- and water-damage control systems.

- These technologies require large support staffs of personnel who are highly skilled in relatively narrow technical disciplines.

- Third-party business and system applications are commercially available from only a relatively limited number of vendors. License fees are generally based on hardware capacity and are expensive. For example, the mainframe version of a $1000 functionally equivalent personal computer database management product can cost between $100,000 and $400,000.

- The performance characteristics of multiuser systems often result in significant upgrade costs to support small incremental increases in demand as total system capacity is approached.

Distributed Single-User Architecture

This approach designs an application so that all functional and data components of the application reside on a single computing platform (Fig. 1.2) dedicated to the use of only one person at a time. The most common examples of applications using this approach are those which we generally categorize as personal productivity aids and include word processing, spreadsheets, graphics, and personal database applications.

A variation of this approach, made possible by the development of local area networking technology, allows single-user applications to provide a limited form of simultaneous shared

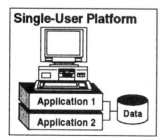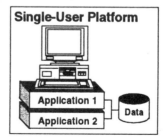

Figure 1.2   Isolated single-user architecture.

access to data across the platforms interconnected by the network. Implementations of this variation (Fig. 1.3) can take many forms, depending on the capabilities of the local area networking technology being used, but the application's architecture is still essentially single-user. The application "views" the data as if it were coresident on the same platform as the application and is still designed to be independently executable on a single platform by a single user.

In either its stand-alone or networked versions this approach is the most commonly used architecture for personal productivity applications. The primary factors driving its use are

- The purpose of the application itself as a "personal" tool, used to perform a limited function for a single user without needing to simultaneously provide access to a common shared repository of data.

- The ready availability of powerful, relatively inexpensive, and standardized hardware platforms and operating systems.

- The commercial availability of powerful and inexpensive applications.

The multiuser variation of this approach evolved in response to

- The availability of fast ($\geq$10 Mbits/s) local area network technology, making it possible to inexpensively interconnect multiple single-user computers.

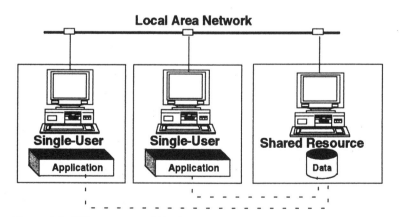

Figure 1.3   File server architecture.

- The need to cost-effectively provide small numbers of users (2 to 50) with shared access to a common repository of data that is typically much smaller than those supported by centralized multiuser applications.
- The inability of corporate MIS departments to develop and deploy smaller applications in a responsive and cost-effective manner.

Strengths

- The technology is based on industry-wide standards and is compatible across a wide range of OEM vendors at very reasonable cost and is also stable and reliable as it is based on standardized and commonly available hardware and software.
- The alternatives available provide the ability to more exactly match processing capacity with demand and are highly scalable, allowing processing capacity to be incrementally increased in a cost-effective manner to keep pace with increases in demand.
- The hardware and system software technologies are simple to understand, use, and maintain, and do not require large staffs of highly skilled technical personnel to provide operational support.
- Literally thousands of reasonably priced third-party applications, across hundreds of categories, are commercially available from a large number of sources.
- Third-party applications are generally designed and developed to be easily used by nontechnical users.
- The user is in complete and total control of the environment.

Weaknesses

- The technologies and applications are targeted to support a single user. Sharing of data, applications, or other resources across many users is difficult and often unreliable.
- Networking and operating system technologies are relatively unsophisticated and do not provide the control and manage-

ment facilities or stability and reliability of more mature multiuser technologies.

■ The environment is inherently multivendor, with one or more OEMs providing the hardware, another providing the operating system, one or more others providing networking technology, and many others providing applications. This significantly increases the environment's operational and administrative complexity and, if implemented in an uncontrolled fashion, can lead to serious enterprise-wide support and reliability problems.

Client/Server Architecture as a Design Approach

This approach designs an application so that the functional components of an application are partitioned in a manner that allows them to be spread across, and executed on, multiple different computing platforms sharing access to one or more common repositories of data (Fig. 1.4).

Client/server architecture is therefore a design approach that distributes the functional processing of an application across two or more different processing platforms. The phrase "client/server" reflects the roles played by the application's functions as they interact with one another. One or more of these functions provide a service, most commonly a database server, that is commonly used by other functions across the application(s). When providing such a service, these functions

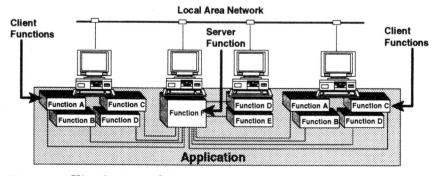

Figure 1.4 Client/server architecture.

are identified as playing a "server" role in the application. Functions that request a "service" from another are playing a "client" role within the application.

It is important to remember that these are roles being played by the functions and not necessarily attributes of the functions themselves. It is quite possible for a specific function to be capable of playing both a client "role" and a "server" role in terms of its interaction with other functions. Consider such common examples as Sybase's Open Server or IBM's DRDA (Distributed Relational Data Architecture) facilities. In these instances the database server function acts as a gateway to another database server (Fig. 1.5) and therefore simultaneously plays both the role of server to the application and client to the remote database server.

Client/server applications are just beginning to come into use in either commercial forms or as proprietary business applications developed by internal management information system (MIS) staff. These client/server applications are most commonly database applications but any application that decomposes its functions in a manner that they play client and/or server roles across different platform boundaries can be accurately described as a client/server application. Examples of currently available client/server applications include electronic-mail (e-mail) applications that feature administration and store/forward server functions, shared networked communication servers, and shared network fax (facsimile) servers. Workgroup applications, a whole new category of software just beginning to become available, that provide shared communications, sched-

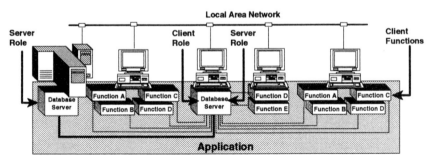

Figure 1.5 Client and server roles.

uling, workflow routing, and a variety of other functions, are also being built on a client/server architectural foundation.

In this book I will focus on the development of database-oriented client/server applications. It is through a more economical and more effective approach to building mainstream line-of-business database applications that I believe the client/server alternative to mainframe-centric systems offers the greatest potential benefit.

2

Benefits, Promises, and Obstacles

Examine recent current trends in the computer industry as a whole. There can be no disputing the fact that proprietary technologies, on which the centralized multiuser architectures are based, are in rapid decline. Once fast-growing minicomputer manufacturers have either disappeared or are in bankruptcy. Others are suffering financial difficulties and struggling to bring new, nonproprietary technologies to market. IBM recently reported the first operating loss in its history and is facing a shrinking market for its mainframe technology. These trends indicate that there is a paradigm shift under way, driven primarily by the rapidly increasing power and decreasing cost of nonproprietary technology solutions and the flexibility offered by the client/server approach in the implementation of these technologies. But what are the benefits that are driving this paradigm shift? What are the obstacles to be faced when transitioning to this new approach? In this chapter we will quantify the more significant of these benefits and discuss the obstacles that are faced by those enterprises wishing to achieve them.

Benefits

Why is the client/server approach generating so much excitement across the industry? Why is it so rapidly supplanting the centralized multiuser approach as the standard approach to developing applications? Industry hype aside, the client/server approach offers very real and tangible benefits to those who successfully make the transition to this new approach. The more significant of these benefits are flexibility, scalability, technological potential, and cost.

Flexibility

Designed and built to service all the processing for hundreds or thousands of simultaneous users, multiuser mainframe architectures tend to exhibit a performance characteristic that seriously impacts the architecture's ability to flexibly handle increasing workload. Multiuser mainframe performance, as measured by response time versus workload (i.e., simultaneous users), tends to remain consistent until the system's design capacity is approached. As workload increases beyond 70 to 80 percent of design capacity, performance degrades rapidly in a nonlinear fashion.

As illustrated in Fig. 2.1, this characteristic limits the flexibility of the multiuser mainframe architecture to cost-effectively provide computing services throughout a wide range of demand. For example, if Fig. 2.1 illustrated the performance characteristics of an entry-level multiuser system whose design capacity was 200 users and cost $2 million per year to install and support, the cost per user to provide response time of 2 sec-

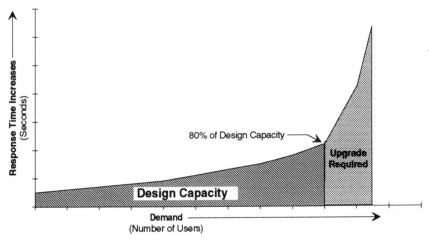

Figure 2.1 Multiuser architecture performance characteristics.

onds or less to 200 users would be $10,000 per user. Decreasing demand by 50 percent (i.e., 100 users) results in essentially the same performance but doubles the per user cost. Increasing demand by only 10 percent beyond design capacity (i.e., 20 new users) doubles the response time experienced by all users. Increasing capacity to provide the original response, in accordance with typical mainframe upgrade policies, can easily double the per user cost for everyone.

Client/server architectures exhibit significantly different performance characteristics because the application's processing is distributed across many different platforms, with only limited and well-defined server processing being performed on "shared" resources. As illustrated in Fig. 2.2, this factor results in a performance curve that is more predictably linear throughout and beyond the individual server platform's design capacity.

The cost per user is more predictable and also increases in a linear fashion. Furthermore, because of the inherent scalability of the architecture, capacity can be added in much smaller, and therefore less costly, increments.

Scalability

Scalability is a characteristic that describes how easily a given system solution can be scaled upward to maintain acceptable response as demand increases. Closely associated with the per-

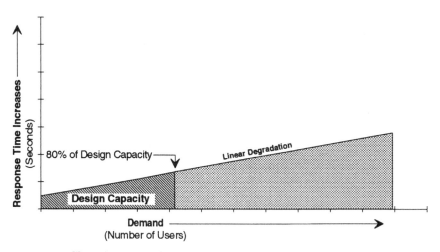

Figure 2.2   Client/server architecture performance characteristics.

formance characteristics of the foundation technologies, this characteristic also factors in the availability of alternatives for increasing capacity. This is another area where client/server architectures, based on open-industry standard technologies, are superior to the proprietary technologies of a multiuser architecture. In a proprietary multiuser environment the customer's upgrade alternatives are limited to what the OEM or, in some cases, a plug-compatible manufacturer (PCM) provides. Quite often, in a captive market, the decision of what alternatives will be available are not driven by customer need or technology but by market and revenue considerations. This results in an often artificial limitation in the alternatives made available as the OEM/PCM seeks to maintain account control while causing the customer to migrate to larger and larger systems. Because of the proprietary nature of the technology, the customer rarely has any viable alternative.

Contrast this with the open technologies on which client/server architectures are based. In this environment the market rules and the customer has many alternatives available for adding processing capacity in incremental steps that are more finely tuned and appropriate to the customer's needs and not the OEM's revenue stream. It is easily possible today to cost-effectively scale a client/server application's capacity from 5 users to well over 200 users in small increments that precisely match increasing demand at an appropriate cost. Further, at the rate of technological change we are currently witnessing, this scalability will soon extend this range to well over 1000 users and the primary limiting factor will be network throughput.

Technological potential

Multiuser architectural technologies have, since their inception, been proprietary. Because of this, technological advances have been controlled and directed by a small number of original equipment manufacturers who experience little, if any, competition in their market segments. Further, the high cost of research, development, and production of proprietary new technologies has historically resulted in relatively long product life cycles. Combine these factors with a very real financial need to protect customer technology investments while maintaining revenue streams, and the results are an incremental and evolutionary increase in processing capacity.

Compare this with the capacity increases experienced by the technology on which the client/server approach is based. The enabling technologies have been driven by intense competition among a large number of OEMs across the entire range of supporting technologies, from central processing units (CPUs) to memory to disk drives to complete systems. Market dynamics and intensive competition have driven shorter and shorter product cycles, while existing and emerging industry-wide standards have relieved customer concerns about protecting technology investments. In combination, these factors have resulted in an explosive growth in processing capacity, product life cycles that are measured in months instead of years, and price/performance ratios that proprietary technologies will never be able to approach.

Cost

Once again the market's influence is a primary determining factor. With an installed base acting as essentially a captive market, there is little competitive pressure for proprietary OEMs to compete on cost. The primary OEM consideration in a captive market is to calculate a price point marginally below the customer's cost to migrate to another proprietary technology. In the market for client/server technology OEMs must compete not just on technological innovation but also on price. Further, much of the technology is standard and the differences between OEM offerings are relatively small. Because of this, pricing tends to become the dominant means of differentiating product. We have seen this trend accelerate as even such major manufacturers as IBM and Compaq are being forced to drastically lower prices and open new distribution channels in order to regain market share lost to their lower-priced competitors.

Obstacles

These benefits are real and tangible, and promise to dramatically lower the processing cost per user. But these benefits do not come easily or without their own costs. Genuine paradigm shifts, which are essentially revolutionary not evolutionary, are often disruptive and the transition painful. Those enterprises seeking to realize the benefits of this new approach to application development must overcome a number of serious obstacles.

Maturity

The nonproprietary technologies which serve as the primary foundation for client/server architectures are relatively immature in comparison to those proprietary technologies on which the centralized multiuser architecture is based. This relative immaturity extends across the entire range of hardware, networking, operating system, and development tools. Although rapidly evolving, these technologies, most of which are less than 10 years old, just do not yet offer the stability of proprietary technologies that have evolved gradually over the last 20 to 30 years.

Complexity

The openness of nonproprietary technologies, while their greatest strength, leads to solutions inherently more complex than those offered by proprietary technologies. Client/server environments are uniformly multivendor, requiring the application developer to integrate often incompatible hardware, software, and networking components from multiple different sources into a single seamless application solution. This factor impacts every aspect of the system's life cycle, from initially selecting appropriate technologies through production operation of the resulting solution. The application developer working in a proprietary centralized multiuser environment is generally concerned only with the application's functionality, not the underlying technology. The task of the client/server developer is far more complex, extending beyond the functionality of the application into the low-level technical details of the environment.

Reliability

Traditional centralized multiuser installations often boast 99.9 percent availability 24 hours a day, 7 days a week. Client/server installations currently cannot approach this level of reliability and it may be years before the technologies have matured to the point where they can. Driven by both the immaturity of the foundation technologies and the complexity of the resulting solutions, client/server applications are inherently less stable and reliable than centralized multiuser applications. Client/server environments have far more points of potential failure than do centralized multiuser environments. Further, the market for client/server technology favors technical innovation over reliable operation, and the manufacturers have responded accordingly. Another factor further impacting reliability is that it is often difficult to identify the reason for a failure and determine which vendor is responsible for fixing the problem. This leads to longer periods of downtime as problems are tracked down and fixed.

Vendor support

Vendors of proprietary technologies have traditionally been known for providing excellent technical and consultative support to their customers. This has long been regarded as a justification for choosing a proprietary approach and is often viewed by the vendors as their primary competitive weapon in maintaining account control over their customer's purchasing decisions. The cost to provide this level of support is subsidized in large part by the high price of the technology.

Vendors of nonproprietary technology, on the other hand, having to compete on price, do not have the margins to subsidize the same high level of support and also recognize that it is very difficult to maintain account control in an open market . Consequently, client/server technologies tend to be poorly supported by their vendors. Although slowly improving, it is highly unlikely that client/server technologies will ever enjoy the level of vendor support that has traditionally been provided by proprietary technologies.

Skills and training

A client/server developer can be accurately viewed as more of a generalist than their mainframe counterpart and needs to have a more broadly based and deeper understanding of the enabling technologies. Further, many of these enabling technologies are new and/or rapidly evolving. It takes time for existing mainframe developers to develop these skills and gain hands-on experience in the integration of these new technologies, and, as the client/server approach is relatively new, the pool of developers who already have these skills and experience is relatively small.

Management tools

Although the number and sophistication of commercially available client/server development tools is rapidly increasing, the same cannot be said for that category of software that supports the operation and management of a production data processing environment. Within most centralized multiuser environments there are a wealth of tools and utilities that have evolved over the years to control, monitor, and manage the reliable operation of the environment. Network management, performance monitoring and tuning, capacity planning, security, disk space allocation and optimization, cost allocation and chargeback, and production job monitoring are only a few of the activities for which such utilities are available. The availability of similar utilities for client/server environments is very limited at the current time and in some cases does not exist at all, making it difficult for system administrators to provide adequate levels of reliability.

Politics

This is quite possibly the greatest single obstacle to be overcome in transitioning from centralized multiuser systems to client/server systems. As with any paradigm shift, an enormous amount of inertia must be overcome before the new paradigm is accepted. Many people do not like change, and this is as true for system developers as it is for any other group. Technical staff have spent their entire careers developing extensive expertise in relatively narrow areas, system managers have made their reputations delivering applications on centralized multiuser technologies, and MIS directors have built large and expensive empires on proprietary technologies that take hundreds of technical staff to operate and support.

The client/server approach, although offering very real and tangible benefits to the enterprise, is often perceived as a threat to the careers of the very people who are tasked with implementing them. The technical expertise gained through years of study and experience is suddenly not as valuable as it was, job security is threatened, and MIS management often equates shrinking budgets and staff with loss of status. Further, the very nature of client/server technologies inevitably delivers greater control into the hands of the end user, a trend that traditional data centers have been fighting for years. These human factors combine to create the most serious obstacle to successful client/server implementation.

Technological Foundations

3

The Foundations

From the developer's perspective, one of the more important differences between typical proprietary multiuser applications and nonproprietary client/server applications is the greater knowledge of the foundation technologies required. The developer of traditional multiuser applications is generally much more insulated from the foundation technologies used to support and deliver the application to the business user. For example, the typical application developer in a large IBM mainframe environment, as illustrated in Fig. 3.1, knows little about the intricacies of the operating system, transaction monitor, telecommunication access method, or the network. With the application's external interaction limited to components (i.e., database and transaction monitor) within a single environment, the developer's technical knowledge need extend no further than the interaction with those components. The developer

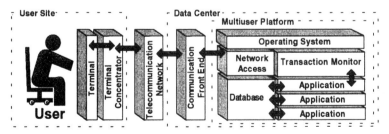

Figure 3.1 Traditional multiuser system architecture.

can function quite adequately while remaining in blissful ignorance of all the other layers actually between the application and the application's user.

Developing client/server applications based on nonproprietary client/server technologies, at least at their current level of maturity, requires a much more thorough knowledge of the environment as a whole. As illustrated in Fig. 3.2, the application itself is now physically separated from the database by layers of components supplied by different vendors that often interact in strange and wondrous ways. Further, the application itself is physically located on the user's platform, a hardware and software environment that is essentially controlled by the user and not a team of highly technical staff overseen by change control committees and the other organizational infrastructures that have evolved to meet the needs of typical large data centers. The developer can no longer assume that everything will work as specified, and when problems arise, as they inevitably will, the developer has to be knowledgeable enough to identify where those problems occurred.

Even with emerging standards, increasing reliability, and the rapidly evolving maturity of these technologies, it will probably be years before the application developer can once again assume that every layer between the user, the application, and the remote functions that the application depends on will work as advertised. To be successful in a client/server environment, application developers must be more of generalists than their typical mainframe counterparts and should invest more time in constantly acquiring new skills and knowledge. Client/server developers cannot rely on expertise in a single language, transaction monitor, and database management system to see them

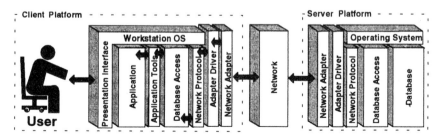

Figure 3.2 Client/server architecture.

through 20 years and retirement. The complexity is too great and the rate of change too fast.

The good news is that client/server developers do not have to be experts in every facet of their environment, only sufficiently knowledgeable to understand the interactions between the components. In most client/server development project teams there will, hopefully, be pools of deep technical expertise to draw on to set up and maintain the environment and troubleshoot problems as they arise. But the developer, as the person directly responsible for delivering the application, must be able to recognize the symptoms of a problem and either take corrective action independently or call on the appropriate pool of expertise. Further, it is the developer who has the closest contact with the end user, and never forget, it is the end user who exercises actual control over the "client" environment.

It is not my intent to make you, the reader, an expert in each of the technologies that serve as the foundation for client/server applications. There are many fine references that cover each technology in far greater detail than I could provide in this book. My intent in this chapter is to provide the developer with a basic understanding of the environment in which the application will operate and, for those who need to build the foundation, with awareness of the options, considerations, and issues that will influence the selection of the technologies on which that foundation must be established.

Selecting Appropriate Technologies

If your organization has a fully established client/server environment, the technology selection process has already been accomplished, for good or ill, and your problem as a developer is greatly simplified. If, on the other hand, you are starting either from scratch or with only a few of the technologies in place, you will, hopefully, become involved in the selection process.

There are many alternatives available for each of the technologies which make up the foundation and those selected are ultimately dependent on the functionality required by business. It is critically important to evaluate and select client/server technologies that function together as a whole to responsively meet the organization's needs. The overriding concern should be matching the capability required to the functionality delivered. Too often, in both large and small organizations, selection of client/server technologies tends to be driven by either cost, politics, and/or adherence to some predefined set of standards chiseled in stone by a committee of technical experts who haven't talked with an end user in years and have no idea what the end user actually does.

This tendency is often most prevalent in large organizations with well-established management information systems and computer services divisions that have evolved to support centralized multiuser mainframe systems. The prime directive of typical large data center management is to ensure uptime through a stable and reliable data-processing environment. It is often believed, with some validity, that this objective can be met only by rigidly controlling (with *controlling* being a euphemism for maintaining the status quo) change. Unfortunately, this inevitably leads to conflict between the established order, often responsible for selecting, installing, and supporting new technologies, and the client/server developer who is ultimately responsible for delivering the application.

Adhering to corporate standards—especially in large organizations where thousands of end users must be supported—is important, but special care must be exercised to keep such standards current and not allow them to become an obstacle to getting the job done. The pace of technological change, in every area of client/server technology, is too rapid for any set of detailed standards to be appropriate for long, and standards that are too general will not meet the need to guarantee stability, interoperability, and support. It is an interesting problem that, unfortunately, has no single "right" answer.

The ultimate objective of the technology selection process is to build a foundation made up of components that will work together reliably to deliver the client/server application to the end user. I have seen a number of different strategies used with varying degrees of success to build the foundations required by client/server applications.

At one extreme is the "buy everything from the same vendor" strategy. Often followed by the "risk-sensitive" established order, this strategy seeks to ease into client/server development with the absolute minimum risk to the environment's stability and reliability. After all, it stands to reason that if you buy everything from the same vendor, it will all work together, won't it? Further, it simplifies the problem immensely. This strategy can work in many situations, and its success hinges on two factors: picking the "right" vendor and having an immense budget. Unfortunately, this approach often results in a solution that does not deliver the client/server benefits of flexibility, cost, and "openness." This approach makes you almost as much a captive of a single vendor as a wholly proprietary centralized multiuser solution while foregoing the stability and reliability benefits of the older, more stable technology. Further, this approach is based on three basic assumptions which tend, in the real world, not to be true.

- There are vendors who can deliver *appropriate* solutions for every needed component.
- Buying everything from the same vendor and/or following their recommendations religiously guarantees trouble-free interoperability.
- Your organization's best interests are the vendor's only concern.

For this strategy to work you must keep two things in mind at all times:

1. Never believe anything a vendor tells you until you've verified it through at least three other customers of that vendor who are using exactly the same components.
2. The vendor's first and highest priority objective is profit. Your organization's best interests are somewhere down the list, if they are on the list at all.

At the other extreme is the "best possible alternative" strategy of selecting the technologically most advanced alternative of each required technology. This is a favorite of technologists who appear to have a psychological need to be constantly on the "leading edge." This strategy seeks to provide the greatest possible functionality, whether needed today or not, while minimizing the risk of future obsolescence by placing bets on emerging technologies. This approach is also based on a number of assumptions that tend not to be true.

- The "best" technologies will interoperate reliably.
- Today's "best" technologies will be tomorrow's "best" technologies.
- The future (3 to 5 years) functionality needed by the organization can be adequately described today.
- The organization's technologists are truly qualified to place long-term technology bets.
- The organization has sufficient technical resources and time to commit to making sure everything works together reliably.

As I stated previously, I have seen both of these strategies succeed and fail in varying situations. But, as in most human endeavors, moderation is usually the key to success, and a strategy that falls somewhere between these two extremes is one that has the best chance of establishing a strong foundation of technologies on which stable and reliable client/server applications can be delivered to the end user. It is difficult to find a "correct" balance between cost, capability, and the organization's needs, and that "ideal" balance point will be different in every organization. As an aid to evaluating the effectiveness of your own selection efforts, consider the graph in Fig. 3.3. This graph plots the relationship between the major factors that tend to influence technology selection and in my experience has proved to be an effective predictor of the ultimate effectiveness

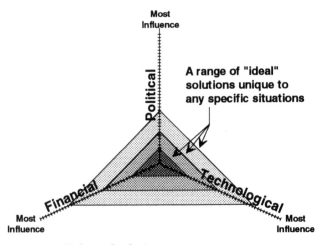

Figure 3.3   Balanced solutions.

of the technology selection process in both large and small organizations moving toward client/server architectures. The "Political" axis measures the influence of such political factors as organizational predetermination (e.g., "We've always been a ____shop and we always will be!!!!!!!!"), receptivity to change, pragmatic acceptance of what works, and risk tolerance on the selection process. The "Financial" axis measures the sensitivity to cost on the selection process, and the "Technological" axis measures the capability and potential of the technologies being seriously considered.

The ideal solutions, for any given environment, will generally be those that show the best balance between these conflicting influences. Unbalanced influences on the selection process will not generally result in suitable or appropriate selections. For example, Figs. 3.4 and 3.5 illustrate technology selection processes that are too influenced by either political, financial, or technology considerations. It is highly unlikely that the resulting selections of either of these processes will cost-effectively meet the needs of the organization or provide a suitable foundation for client/server applications.

As you proceed with the selection process, the criteria you use to evaluate the alternatives will change as the technologies being evaluated change, but there are criteria that are more generally applicable across all choices being evaluated. The fol-

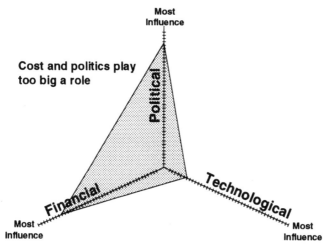

Figure 3.4 Politically unbalanced solutions.

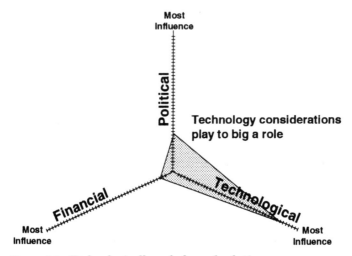

Figure 3.5 Technologically unbalanced solutions.

lowing illustrate a set of such guidelines that are meant to foster the flexibility and openness that I believe are the most important characteristics of a client/server architecture while minimizing as much as possible the risks inherent in the migration process.

Functionality.   Always the most important criterion, this seeks to identify the alternative that most closely matches the capability provided with the functionality required.

Flexibility.   Where there is no clearly superior alternative in terms of functionality, select the alternative that least restricts selections in other areas. For example, if two different database management alternatives are essentially equivalent in functionality, pick the one that provides the widest range of development and end-user access tools or that operates on the widest range of hardware and operating system platforms.

Viability.   Where there is no clearly superior alternative in terms of flexibility, examine the future potential of the product in terms of its viability. Does it conform to recognized standards applicable in its area? Is it from a vendor that is financially sound and have a long track record of continuing to evolve and promote their products? Does the product have a significant and growing market share?

Cost.   This should be self-explanatory.

Corporate standards.   If there is still no clearly superior alternative, match the selections against any corporate standards that may be appropriate and pick the one that follows these standards. I realize that many, especially in the corporate MIS world, will think this criterion is the most, not least, important. It has been my experience, though, that in most large organizations any applicable standards that may exist are anywhere from 12 to 18 months out of date. Further, the real question to be answered is: Will the alternative coexist peacefully in the existing environment without introducing unwanted instability and reliability problems? Not whether the alternative adheres to a possibly outdated or inappropriate set of standards that exist merely to maintain the status quo.

Toss a coin.   If, after the preceding steps, there is still no clearly superior alternative toss a coin, make a selection, and get on with your life. Dithering over a close call while arguing endlessly over esoteric fine points is a trap that is all to easy to fall into for technologists. If the decision is that close, it probably doesn't matter, and in the final analysis between any two given alternatives you have only a 50/50 chance of being "right" anyway. Immense amounts of time have been wasted debating irrelevancies [remember EISA (extended industry standard architecture) vs. microchannel] that could have been spent productively building something.

The Foundation Technologies

What technologies form the foundation of a client/server environment? The foundation technologies generally fall into three distinct groups which tend, as illustrated in Fig. 3.6, to overlap actual hardware platform boundaries. This overlap, as I will discuss in Chap. 8, is often the source of many of the organizational problems that confront client/server developers seeking to downsize applications from traditional mainframe-centric environments.

As I discuss these technologies in the following chapters my focus will tend to be limited to those that are generally considered by the corporate business community to be mainstream

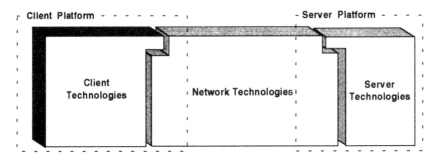

Figure 3.6 Client/server technologies.

and commercially available, or soon to be available, products. There are many fine and often superior technologies in use today, each with their loyal adherents, that for one reason or another have not been able to make the transition from narrow niche or vertical market usage into mainstream general use. Their exclusion from the following chapters is not meant to imply that these are not worthy of mention, only that space and time are limited and no slight to these other alternatives is intended.

4

Client
Technologies

In the majority of client/server applications, the client functions are generally those which are running on the end user's workstation, and for the purposes of this discussion I will focus on the components of the client in this sense of the client role. As illustrated in Fig. 4.1, the components of the client workstation are the basic workstation hardware, the operating system, the database connectivity software, applications, and, optionally, a graphical-user interface (GUI). I say "optionally" because, although often associated in the user's mind with client/server technology, GUIs are not necessarily implicit in the client/server architecture.

Although more attention is often directed toward server and network technology in the selection process, it is the client, in

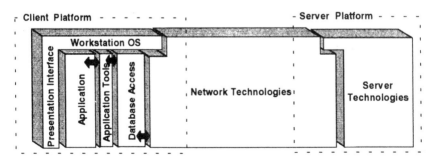

Figure 4.1   Client components.

my opinion, that is the most important of foundation technologies. It is the client environment with which the end user interacts the most intimately. It is the client functions that generally make up the majority of a client/server application, and it is the needs of the client workstation for which the network and the server exist. For these reasons special consideration should be focused on mapping desired end-user functionality to the capability of the client technologies.

Before the selection process is begun, you should have a clear understanding of what functions the end user expects the client workstation to perform. Don't limit your understanding to only the functions a specific client/server application will provide. Look beyond the application to the end user's other activities, and always keep in mind that the workstation is a general-purpose tool that will have other, possibly equally important, roles to play beyond serving as a host to your application.

Applications and Tools

In keeping with the belief that the functionality required is the most important criterion, identify the applications that will need to be provided. Does the user require connectivity to remote mainframe systems? Does the user participate in group communication (e-mail) and scheduling activities? Will general office functions (word processing, spreadsheets, graphics, etc.) need to be provided? Are specialized vertical market applications (real-time financial market data, on-line reservation systems, etc.) needed?

Another aspect that is critically important, from the developer's viewpoint, is the availability of application development tools. These tools include the various computer languages, text editors, debuggers, design aids, and all the other miscellaneous tools that make it possible to design, develop, test, and deliver a client/server application. It is the client workstation on which the application will ultimately reside, and, in most cases, an equivalent to that workstation is what the developer will be using to build that application.

Discussion of client applications highlights another major difference between client/server development and traditional mainframe development. In traditional mainframe development the application itself is usually thought of as being relatively self-contained, using primarily a single language and database and executing within a specific production region [CICS (Customer Information Control System), IMS (Information Management System), etc.]. Typical mainframe applications do not generally incorporate many different tools, especially end-user-oriented tools, to deliver a wide range of functionality. If such functionality is desired by the end user, the developer might, at most, ship an extract of data into an accessible spot for the user to handle as desired.

Client/server developers, though, must be aware of all the various tools and applications, whether purchased or developed internally, already existing on the client workstation and attempt to leverage the functionality represented by those as much as possible. For example, if there is a requirement for statistical analysis and graphical display, it makes little sense for the developer to "program" that capability into their application if an already existing tool (e.g., a spreadsheet) is already available that can be "incorporated" into the application to provide that same functionality. With the new developments in operating systems and emerging standards in such program-to-program communication mechanisms as dynamic data exchange (DDE), object linking and embedding (OLE), and remote-procedure calls (RPC), such integration can appear seamless to the end user.

End-user tools

Traditionally, applications and tools were generally viewed as falling into clearly delineated categories. The first were such basic productivity applications as word processing, spreadsheets, and presentation tools. These were used by end users to perform their basic administrative and office functions. The second category included those easily used, semiprogrammable tools that facilitated data query and reporting activities. Once again these were considered as primarily end-user tools. Then there were the applications that have come to be considered as workgroup applications, or those that facilitated communication among end users, with electronic mail being the most prevalent example. Finally, there were the "real" development tools, used only by "professional" application developers. These were the full-featured computer languages, compilers, text editors, debuggers, and other miscellaneous tools used by the developer to build production applications.

The distinctions between these categories are rapidly disappearing. With the incorporation of increasingly functional macrolanguages and more easily used ways to link applications together, products that were previously dismissed as "productivity" aids are approaching the capabilities needed by "professional" application development. "Professional" developers who still view such tools as toys should take a walk around their organizations and see what non-data-processing personnel are doing with their word-processing or spreadsheet macros.

Developer tools

As what were once thought of as productivity tools are becoming more capable, professional development tools are becoming far more easily used. Over the last 3 years we have seen an explosion of new, powerful, and easily used full-scale professional development tools that are easily equal or superior to any tool available to traditional mainframe developers. Although the line between professional development tools and traditional productivity applications is blurring, there are still a number of characteristics that serve to distinguish the suitability of a tool for professional development use, especially in the development of what are commonly thought of as line-of-business or mission-crucial applications.

- A professional development tool must be able to support large multiperson development efforts by facilitating the sharing and integration of code developed by many developers across one or more projects. Development tools that are totally self-contained and assume "one developer–one application," no matter how capable, are too limited in any sizable project.

- A professional development tool must be able to encapsulate its code into some inaccessible and nonmodifiable form for distribution to end users. This encapsulation can take the form of compilation and linkage into binary executables, compression into forms executable only through run-time libraries, or any other mechanism that serves to protect the application from unauthorized modification.

- A professional development tool, especially in a client/server environment, must be able to access, in as direct a manner as possible, many different types of database servers. Development tools that are tied to a single database management package are, in the long run, too limiting in today's multiple database environment.

- A professional development tool must be able to take full advantage of the features and facilities made available to it by the environment in which it operates. If the tool is meant to operate within an environment offering a graphical-user interface, it must take full advantage of that interface in standard ways. If program-to-program communication facilities are provided (DDE, OLE, RPC, etc.), the tools must be able to utilize those facilities.

Any development tool that can meet these basic constraints should, I believe, be considered a professional development tool. Unfortunately, as developers are essentially technologists at heart, there is probably no other technology that can generate as heated a discussion as the relative merits of the various tools and languages available today. After spending years acquiring expertise in a given computer language or tool, whether a low-level tool like "C" or one of the newer high-level tools, developers do not like to walk away from that expertise and start over again. This rather human failing often manifests itself as prejudice against newer or more easily used tools as somehow "unfit" for true professionals to use. In your efforts to select an appropriate tool, be aware of this factor and do not allow it to unduly influence the selection process. Further, do not automatically assume that a single tool is all that will be needed or used. When the only tool you have is a hammer, every problem looks like a nail.

Such lower-level compiled languages as FORTRAN, COBOL, and C have, in the past, often had the advantage of being based on national or internationally recognized standards set by groups such as ANSI (American National Standards Institute). This supposedly allowed developers to choose compilers and other tools with minimal risk as their source code could, with minimal trouble, be compatible across various vendor tools. With the fierce competition among vendors offering such tools, the widespread use of extensions to support such new technologies as object orientation that have yet to be codified into a standard, and the availability of proprietary libraries such as the Windows Foundation Classes from Microsoft and Borland's OWL extensions, this advantage is more perceived than real. Higher-level languages, whether compiled or interpreted, often provide equal or superior functionality, greater ease of use, and the promise of more rapid development but are generally proprietary to a single vendor, not based on any recognized standard, and pose a slightly greater risk to the possibility of obsolescence or lack of support if the vendor fails. The tradeoffs are generally obvious and the risk can be managed with appropriate attention to the stability and viability of the vendor.

A further consideration is the relationship between the client environment and tool selection. Although many tools offer versions for multiple different platforms and, as a market trend, we can expect to see more and more tools being made available across different operating systems, there is still a very intimate and dependent relationship between tools and the client environment's operating system. Generally speaking, the more popular the environment the more tools that will be available. Whichever is weighted more heavily in your own situation will tend to drive and/or limit the selection process in the other. For example, if the client operating system absolutely must be OS/2 for some reason, then only development tools for the OS/2 environment can be considered. If the widespread availability of development tools is more important for some (no doubt equally important) reason, then the operating system decision will probably be weighted toward Microsoft Windows or a Unix variant.

Operating System

The primary purpose of the workstation operating system is to provide applications operating on that workstation with access to the hardware resources (memory, disk data storage, video and printer output, etc.) of that workstation and manage the interfaces between that workstation and devices external to that workstation (video, printer, etc.). Today workstation operating systems are distinguished by four primary technical considerations.

Memory addressability

This is the capability of the operating system to address random-access memory (RAM). Keep in mind that this is not a measurement of how much RAM can be supported by a specific hardware configuration. The actual amount of RAM that can be effectively utilized is a function of the interaction between the operating system and the hardware on which it is operating, but the limiting factor is primarily the operating system. The MS-DOS operating system, designed initially for hardware incapable of addressing more than 1 Mbyte of memory, is effectively limited (despite a number of workarounds) to a 1-Mbyte address space even when operating on hardware configurations capable of supporting more than 256 Mbytes of RAM. Generally speaking, the more memory that can be effectively addressed, the more capable the operating system is and the more powerful applications operating within that operating system can be.

Single- vs. multitasking

This is the characteristic that determines the ability of the operating system to load and execute applications in what appears to be a simultaneous manner. I say "appears to be simultaneous" because any computer with a single central processing unit (CPU) can, with a very few exceptions, execute only a single instruction at a time. But each of these instructions is performed very quickly. Further, it is often the case that the CPU has to wait on other, slower, components such as disk drives before it can perform the next task. A multitasking operating system takes advantage of these two characteristics to execute instructions from one application while another application is waiting for other tasks to be completed, therefore giving the impression that multiple applications are executing simultaneously. Multitasking operating systems, are by nature, more functional and capable and are a superior alternative.

There are two basic approaches to multitasking in today's operating system, cooperative and preemptive. In a cooperative approach the applications executing concurrently cooperate among themselves for access to shared system resources [CPU, RAM, I/O (input/output), etc.], each alternatively giving up control of those resources periodically according to established standards and guidelines specific to the operating system. Each application, while it is executing, has complete access to all of the system's resources, and the operating system essentially acts only to facilitate access to those resources.

A preemptive approach has the operating system acting as a "door" to shared resources, forcing all applications to request access to such resources from the operating system. The operating system uses such requests as an opportunity to temporarily "halt" one application while giving access to another, thereby acting as an arbitrator between applications.

Much has been made of the better "stability" of preemptive operating systems, and it is true that preemptive operating systems do tend to be somewhat more stable, but anyone who has worked with OS/2 or Unix for any length of time knows that preemption is no guarantee of stability. Further, when selecting a workstation operating system, you must evaluate just how important absolute stability is to the expected use of that workstation. What is the worst-case scenario if the operating system crashes? How much work will be lost? How many people will be impacted? How long does it take to recover from the crash? A system crash for a mainframe computer servicing thousands of users is a disaster. For most workstation usage, a system crash is an inconvenience that impacts only one person and can be recovered from quickly and easily.

Graphical-user interface facilities

This refers to the ability of the operating system to support, include, or provide the application(s) executing within that operating system with standard application programming interfaces that allow users to interact with both their applications and the operating system itself in a more intuitive and easily used graphical manner that is consistent across all applications residing in that environment. Although client/server applications do not, in and of themselves, have to use a GUI to communicate with the end user, the trend in user interfaces is definitely toward some form of GUI, and client/server applications will almost always utilize such an interface if it is available.

A GUI has two faces and is perceived differently by the end user and the application developer. The end user perceives the GUI as the "look and feel" of the interface to the system. The developer perceives the GUI as (1) an application programming interface (API) to which the application issues commands to present information to the user and a mechanism to accept commands initiated by the user and (2) a set of guidelines that should be followed in order to ensure that the developer's application will interact with the user in a manner that is consistent with all other applications operating through that GUI.

A GUI can be embedded into, and considered a part of, the operating system itself or provided as extensions to the operating system. Examples of the first approach include the Macintosh operating system from release 1.0 to today's current System 7, the presentation manager of IBM's OS/2 2.x, and the facilities of Windows NT, while examples of the second approach include Microsoft's Windows as an extension of MS-DOS or the various flavors of available Unix GUI facilities (OSF/Motif, Sun's OpenLook, etc.). X-Windows, often mistakenly considered as a Unix GUI, is not a graphical-user interface per se but a low-level API and extensive protocol that governs the interaction between various functions of an application, whether they reside on a single platform or are distributed across many interconnected platforms.

Hardware independence

The final consideration that categorizes operating systems is the degree of independence they offer from specific hardware configurations. Unix, for example, can be thought of as the most "open" and portable of mainstream operating systems. Designed to be portable and written in "C" (possibly the most "portable" of today's programming languages), the Unix operating system has been adapted for practically every type of processor and brand of computer made in the last 20 years. But, taken individually, many Unix implementations are unique and proprietary to a specific OEM and that OEM's hardware and in this respect are almost as "closed" as any fully proprietary hardware/software combination traditionally offered by Digital Equipment, IBM, and others.

MS-DOS, today's most popular workstation operating system, is basically limited to hardware configurations built on the Intel 808x processor family (8086, 8088, 80286, 80386, 80486, etc.) and those from other manufacturers that are fully compatible with these. OS/2 2.x is effectively limited to Intel 80386 and its successors. As literally hundreds of manufacturers provide compatible computer systems based on this architecture, this limitation is not a serious consideration. Remember, it is vendor independence that is a goal of client/server development, not necessarily independence from any given technology.

Unix, as stated previously, is the most portable of today's mainline operating systems, and a number of industry trends are ensuring that this portability increases. The first such trend is the increasingly rapid convergence of previously proprietary Unix versions toward an increasingly standard and more open implementation. The second is the efforts of a number of OEMs to "port" their previously proprietary Unix implementations to other OEMs platforms. Sun's Solaris 2.0 for Intel processors is a prime example of this trend. The third, and possibly most significant, trend is represented by the licensing of existing and newly developed processor architectures by OEMs who have traditionally maintained proprietary control over such technology. Examples of this trend include Sun's SPARC technology and the IBM/Apple/Motorola development of the PowerRisc technology.

And then there are the new operating systems coming down the road, such as Microsoft's Windows-NT and the as yet unnamed next-generation operating system from the joint IBM/Apple Taligent effort. As these trends continue hardware and operating system dependence will become less and less of an issue.

Hardware Platform

This is the basic client technology foundation on which everything else rests. The hardware is what most of us think of as the "computer system." The basic hardware components of the client include the central processing unit (CPU), random-access memory (RAM), direct-access storage devices (DASD, also known as *disk drives*), one or more input devices (keyboards, mice, etc.), and a video monitor. Client workstations are available in proprietary, semiproprietary, and totally open-industry standard packages to meet every known customer need.

Much has been written about the different design approaches taken to the technologies that make up the hardware of a client workstation. The relative merits of reduced instruction set vs. complex instruction set CPUs and the extended industry standard architecture (EISA) vs. microchannel vs. industry standard architecture (ISA) vs. proprietary bus architecture are examples of the most recent areas of dispute. For the purposes of providing a hardware platform on which to build a suitable client/server foundation, these distinctions are rapidly becoming irrelevant. The primary concerns which should drive the selection process are functional, not technical, and involve asking the following:

- Will the platform, as a whole, be fast enough to responsively meet the needs of the end user?

- Does the platform support one or more operating systems for which there are a wide selection of applications available to meet the functional requirements of the end user?

- Is the platform "closed" or "open"? "Closed" platforms are proprietary to a single OEM who acts as the sole source for that technology, while "open" platforms are based on industry standard technologies that are available from a number of OEMs. Open technologies are generally preferable to closed, all other factors being equal, if only to minimize the risk associated with obsolescence and OEM financial failure. But all other factors are rarely equal, and for any given situation a proprietary closed platform can sometimes offer advantages that outweigh the disadvantages.

- Does the platform cost-effectively meet the functional needs of the end user? It makes little sense to provide a $20,000 workstation to someone performing basic office administration, data entry, and communication tasks. Unfortunately, management often looses sight of the fact that it makes even less sense to scrimp on a tool as potentially important as the end-user workstation. For example, the difference between the functional capabilities and responsiveness of $2500 and $5000 workstations can be immense, but the incremental cost over 3 years is less than $70 per month.

Database Access

This component provides the application with an interface to which database access requests, most often formatted as structured query language (SQL) statements, are submitted and verified and through which server responses are returned. SQL, as the only recognized standard (or semistandard) mechanism for accessing data across a variety of database engines, is the current lingua franca of client/server database applications, and its emergence as a standard is in large part responsible for the popularity and growth in client/server computing.

At its most basic, the database access component consists of two parts, as illustrated in Fig. 4.2. The first is the component to which the application passes its requests and from which it receives its data. The second component is responsible for preparing the verified and formatted SQL statement with any interprocess communication protocol-specific statements, such as OS/2's named pipes or Unix RPC calls, that may be required to establish or maintain linkage with the database, and then formatting the resulting request in the manner expected by the network's transport protocol. There are two basic approaches to providing the SQL API portion of this access.

Embedded SQL

At the most basic level almost all databases support two different approaches to providing this access capability. The first is usually referred to as *embedded SQL* because the programmer embeds the SQL code directly into the program as normal program statements delineated by EXEC SQL and END-SQL statements. The syntax for this is common across most precompilers offered by database vendor convention and is based on IBM's DB/2 conventions, which act as a sort of de facto standard. In this approach the programmer writes the SQL code directly into the program in line with the program's other code,

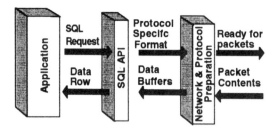

Figure 4.2 Database connectivity.

with the SQL code delineated by some identifying statements that defined the starting and ending points of the SQL code block. For example,

```
                Program Code
                     .
                     .
EXEC SQL
    SELECT CUST_NBR, CUST_NAME
    INTO CUSTOMER-NBR, CUSTOMER-NAME
    FROM CUSTOMER
    WHERE CUST_NBR = 123
END-SQL
                Program Code
```

The resulting program is then scanned by software called a *precompiler* provided by the database vendor. A precompiler is specialized software which scans the source code being input into a compiler and replaces certain statements with their equivalent in-line assembly language or function call statements, which can then be compiled by the actual compiler and linked into executable code specific to the environment for which the program is being prepared. In the case of a SQL precompiler the embedded SQL statements are most generally replaced with function call statements to a data access function library provided by the database vendor. This approach offers several advantages: the first is the relative simplicity and straightforwardness of the program's interface with the database.

The second advantage is the relative portability of the resulting program. Because the majority of precompilers use a common de facto standard syntax and most database vendors comply with at least level 1 of the ANSI SQL standard, a little care on the developer's part can result in an application that merely needs to be "recompiled" using a different compiler and database function library to be portable across operating systems and database management systems. The primary disadvantage of this approach is that precompilers are generally made available for only a few highly standardized compiled languages such as COBOL, FORTRAN, and C. Newer, more proprietary, and less standard development tools are generally barred from using this approach.

Function call interface

The second approach involves directly accessing the function library, again provided by the database vendor, with function calls through which the application passes SQL statements and then retrieving the results of the request through additional functional calls which act to bind the data into the specified program variables. The example below illustrates this complexity in comparison to embedded SQL using "generic" function calls to illustrate the difference. Keep in mind that the following are not actual function calls but are representative examples of those typical to different database management systems. (*Note:* SQL commands are in **BOLD** capital letters; program variables in upper- and lowercase.)

```
First you have to open a connection and get a "handle":
    SqlHandle=SQLCONNECT(Login_Variables, Database_Name)

Then you have to build the query in the query buffer:
    Sql_Statement="Select Cust_Nbr, Cust_Name from
Customer"
    Sql_Statement=Sql_Statement+"Where Cust_Nbr=123"
    SQLCOMMAND (SqlHandle, Sql_Statement)

Then you have to execute the command to the database:
    SQLEXEC (SqlHandle)

Then you bring the results back to the client buffers:
    SQLGETDATA (SqlHandle)

Then you process each row returned:
```

```
DO UNTIL SQLFETCHNEXTROW(SqlHandle) = -1
For each row returned bind each column to a program variable
    Customer_Nbr=SQLBINDDATA (SqlHandle, 1)
    Customer_Name=SQLBINDDATA (SqlHandle, 2)
    Record oriented program processing
        ...........
        ..........
LOOP
```

This approach results in more complex programs because the program is handling all the lower-level details previously handled by the precompiler. Another disadvantage to this approach is that function libraries, without either de facto or formal standards to guide them, tend to be highly unique and specific to database management systems. This approach does offer some advantages. The first is that it can be used by any programming language or development tool that can initiate a function call, which is practically everything from desktop application macrolanguages to C. The second advantage is that, with direct access to the function library, the application has greater flexibility in the type and nature of information it can retrieve about the database itself. The last advantage can be performance. Depending on the efficiency and "smarts" of the supplied precompiler, it is possible for the programmer to produce more efficient database access code by directly accessing the function library.

Higher-level development tool approaches

Higher-level proprietary development tools often shield, to a large extent, the application developer from the complexities of interfacing directly with the database-specific function library by providing the developer with simpler more easily used mechanisms to access data in a more generic manner that is not specific to a given database server. These mechanisms can range from "pointing and clicking" on database fields to being able to embed SQL statements directly into the code in a manner similar to the approach used by precompilers. The development tool itself then takes care of initiating the function calls and retrieving the data into program variables.

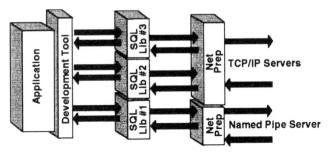

Figure 4.3   Development tool layer.

At the cost of making the environment more complex, this approach significantly simplifies the programmer's job and isolates the application even further from changes in that environment. As illustrated in Fig. 4.3, most such tools are designed to work with many different database servers without any change to the application itself. Some, such as Powerbuilder from Powersoft, Inc., even make it possible to simultaneously access multiple different database servers from different vendors, thus consolidating the data of multiple incompatible databases into a single view for the user. This is something that is nearly impossible to do in lower-level development tools using either precompilation or function calls without adding a significant amount of essentially redundant complexity and overhead to your application.

Middleware

The need to provide applications with greater independence from the database function libraries has led to the development of third-party function libraries and other tools that essentially stand between the application, irrespective of the language it is developed in, and the foundation function libraries unique to each database. Pioneer Software's Q&E Database Library and Multi-Link products fall into this category. These products are architected very similarly to the higher-level language approach illustrated in Fig. 4.3 but are independent of any specific database or language. Q&E Database Library, for example, makes it possible to access over 20 major relational and nonrelational databases with exactly the same function library calls and SQL code.

Industry standards

A relatively recent development in the client/server arena is the emerging standard associated with function-level call interfaces. Thanks in large part to the efforts of the SQL access group, a group created to establish and administer industry-wide standards related to the SQL language and relational databases, a call-level interface (CLI) standard specification has been put forward and Microsoft's Open Database Connectivity (ODBC) standard API has been developed in accordance with this specification and has been freely licensed to relational database software vendors and third-party providers who are working to bring database-specific versions of this common call interface to market.

A functionally enhanced, but essentially compatible, API called the *integrated database application programming interface* (IDAPI) has been proposed to the SQL access group for consideration by a number of software vendors led by Borland International, Inc. Both are architected in a similar manner, partitioning the database access mechanism into two functionally independent modules, as illustrated in Fig. 4.4, one of which provides a standardized call-level interface to the application, while the second takes and converts the call-level interface (CLI) into database-specific SQL commands to pass directly to the database engine.

Although ODBC drivers are not yet widely available and IDAPI extensions to the standard SAG CLI specification have not yet been approved, both of these developments are good news and promise to further isolate the application from the database without forcing the developer to use a proprietary language for the sole purpose of providing this isolation.

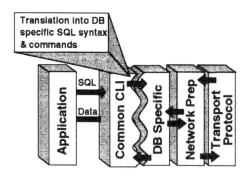

Figure 4.4   ODBC architecture.

Interprocess Communication Protocols

As SQL is the common "language" that allows applications to be isolated from but communicate with various relational database products, interprocess communications protocols (IPCs) are the common "language" that allows any two programs running in the same or different environment to send and receive messages, commands, and responses. The nature of client/server architecture requires a highly developed interprocess communication protocol to control, synchronize, and facilitate the message flow between client and server applications. IPC protocols play a critically important part in the client/server architecture and are generally responsible for:

- Coordinating a transaction session between a "client" process and a "server" process.
- Pacing the transfer of data between the two processes so that each can complete processing of "old" data before "new" data arrives.
- Making the network location of each process "transparent" to the other process.

Named pipes, remote-procedure calls (RPCs), and application program to program communication (APPC) are the three most commonly utilized IPC protocols in today's client/server environments.

Named pipes

Named pipes is the native IPC protocol of OS/2 and is a fully implemented API that provides interprocess communication between programs in a manner that is very similar to writing to a file, except that the "file" is referred to as a "named pipe" that can be shared by many different processes at once. Pipes can be unidirectional (write or read) or bidirectional (write and read), blocking or nonblocking, and dedicated to a single process or used by many processes. An OS/2-specific protocol, named pipes is used extensively by Microsoft's version of SQLServer and, until recently, was the only method through which clients could communicate with an OS/2 SQLServer server.

Remote-procedure calls

RPCs are the interprocess communication protocol primarily used in Unix environments to facilitate program-to-program communication. Although loosely specified by the X-Open standards, RPC protocols have, in the past, been largely proprietary to specific vendors' Unix implementation. With the ongoing consolidation of the Unix world and the closer cooperation between Unix International and the Open Systems Foundation, the various forms of vendor-specific RPCs are becoming more standardized. RPCs are implemented as a compiler feature supported by platform-specific RPC run-time libraries that allows the program to initiate remote-procedure calls in the same manner as a local procedure call would be made with the run-time library responsible for "finding" the remote procedure, establishing the transaction session, and handling all the communication, completely transparently to the application. Primarily a Unix protocol, RPCs are used extensively by Unix-based SQL database products to facilitate the connection between client processes (applications) and server processes (databases).

APPC

APPC is IBM's System Network Architecture (SNA) interprocess communication protocol to facilitate conversational (i.e., transaction-based) communication between logical units (software) executing on physical units (hardware) across an SNA-compliant network. Developed to support interprocess communication across a wide range of heterogeneous IBM host systems operating within an SNA environment, APPC is a functionally rich and powerful protocol that addresses security, remote-program initiation, distributed checkpoints and synchronized half-duplex (i.e., one direction at a time). APPC is supported by IBM Common Programming Interface for Communications (CPI-C) software provided for each IBM-supported platform (DOS, OS/2, OS/400, VM, MVS, etc.). In the client/server architecture APPC is the IPC protocol of choice for client connections to such IBM database management products as OS/2 Data Manager, SQL/400, SQL/DS, and DB/2.

5

Network
Technologies

An explicit characteristic of the client/server architecture is
that there must be a communication linkage between the client
and server platforms across which the client's request for data
and the server's response are communicated. This communication linkage can take many different forms, from dial-up access
over switched public phone lines to the typical dedicated point-
to-point SNA networks found in most large IBM mainframe
environments. While any reliable and fast linkage can support
a client/server application, such linkages tend to be highly specific to the requirements of a given environment, and the more
commonly used approach to establishing connectivity between
clients and servers involves the use of local area networking
technologies. Because these connectivity technologies are so
important to the client/server architecture, I've written this
chapter with the intent of providing the developer with an
overview of the typical components of a local area network
(LAN) and how they interact with the application and the
server to establish and maintain the necessary communication.
This chapter seeks to give the developer a basic background
understanding of the features and components of a local area
network and the roles these play in a client/server architecture.
It will not make you an expert but hopefully allow you to at
least nod in the right place when discussing problems with the
real networking experts.

Local Area Network

A local area network is that collection of networking hardware, cabling, and protocols that work together to provide a method for computers and data systems to connect and share cabling. Protocols, in the context of local area networks, are simply rules that define how these various components will work together at each level. Often, these rules are codified into the public domain by public organizations set up specifically to define and oversee the definition and modification of these standards. In the United States the primary organization tasked with defining such standards is the 802 Committee of the Institute of Electrical and Electronic Engineers (IEEE), who have established specific committees to oversee and administer these standards. The role played by such organizations is pivotal to the industry as it provides a framework within which many different manufacturers can develop and bring to market networking components that will generally work with components from other manufacturers to establish a stable and reliable network.

The two major approaches to local area networking that adhere to standards defined and managed by the IEEE are Ethernet, overseen by the 802.3 subcommittee, and token ring, overseen by the 802.5 subcommittee. Each of these different approaches combine cabling topologies, signaling techniques, information packaging, and access control protocols encompassing the physical and data-link control layers of networking in different ways to meet the objective of being able to pass a packet of information across a local area network.

At its simplest level a packet can be thought of as an envelope that contains information being passed by the network. This envelope carries a destination address for the recipient and a return address for the sender. The ways in which these addresses are specified, the format of the information inside the envelope, and the way the accuracy and completeness of the information are verified are determined by protocols.

Ethernet

Based on inventions of Robert Metcalfe and David Boggs at Xerox PARC [Palo Alto (Calif.) Research Center] and popularized with commercial products from Xerox, DEC, and Intel, the

Ethernet network is the oldest of the standards-based local area networks and has evolved significantly over the years since its introduction in the early 1970s. The definitive operational characteristics of Ethernet are its speed (10 Mbits/s), bus topology, the distance it can cover (approximately 2 mi between nodes), and the means it uses to arbitrate access to the transmission medium, carrier sense multiple access with collision detection (CSMA/CD).

Topology. The standard Ethernet topology is a bus or daisy chain, as illustrated in Fig. 5.1, where each device is attached directly to another device through means of a coax(ial) cable. This cabling scheme offers the advantages of simplicity and low cost at the cost of reliability and flexibility. In terms of reliability the biggest weakness of a bus topology is the fact that a break anywhere in the bus will bring the network down. In terms of flexibility, a bus, although easier to set up initially, becomes increasingly more difficult to configure as new devices are added to the network or existing devices are moved to different locations.

To address some of these problems the 802.3 committee created a standard, referred to as *10BaseT,* defining the use of twisted-pair cabling configured physically as a star topology centered around intelligent hub concentrators, illustrated in Fig. 5.2. The star topology is uniquely suited to the already existing typical telephone wiring schemes in widespread use and significantly increases the flexibility with which new nodes can be attached and existing nodes moved around.

Although physically a star topology, 10BaseT is still, electrically, a bus, and to address the "cable break" weakness of an electrical "bus" the 10BaseT standard calls for an intelligent hub that can detect such a break and automatically drop the

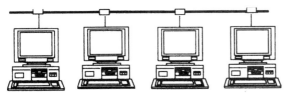

Figure 5.1 Standard Ethernet bus topology.

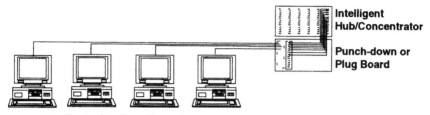

Figure 5.2   Typical 10BaseT topology.

broken cable segment and reconfigure the bus around the break, thus retaining network integrity. Ethernet is limited, in either of its topologies, to a maximum of 1000 nodes on a single network segment.

CSMA/CD. The second defining characteristic of Ethernet is the protocol by which it allows shared transmission access to the cable. Until such new technologies as asynchronous transmission mode become standardized and in more widespread use only a single device can access any baseband network at a time. Media access protocols are thus necessary to allow multiple devices to share a single medium at once. In Ethernet this protocol is called *CSMA/CD* and requires each station to "listen" before it transmits. If the line is "busy," the station must wait until it isn't. If two stations happen to listen at the same time, hear nothing, and transmit simultaneously, the "collision" results in a scrambled message which both stations detect. Each station then waits for a predetermined yet random period and tries to transmit again. Think of CSMA/CD as working just like your telephone. Each person can speak only when the other is listening. If they both happen to speak at once the message is garbled, which both recognize, and each person waits to listen before speaking again.

Token ring

Based on patents awarded to Olof Soderblom of the Netherlands, codified into standards by the IEEE 802.5 subcommittee, and popularized by IBM as their standard local area network, the token ring network is the new guy on the block, being introduced by IBM in the late 1980s. The definitive operational characteristics of token ring are its dual speeds (4 and 16 Mbits/s), star/ring topology, and the means it uses to arbitrate access to the transmission medium, token passing.

Topology. The only topology used by token ring networks is a ring, or complete circle, that is implemented physically as a star using either active (smart) or passive (stupid) hubs called media access units (MAUs), as illustrated in Fig. 5.3. This cabling scheme offers the same advantages of Ethernet's 10BaseT topology. The reliability of token ring networks is not an issue of the topology, as with Ethernet, but of the media access method used.

Although physically a star topology, token ring is electrically a ring with each node being connected to two other nodes, the one to the "left" and the one to the "right," and the electrical connection is a complete unbroken circle. Token ring MAUs are normally eight port concentrators with two additional ports that are specifically used to connect two MAUs together, thereby extending the "ring" to additional devices. A single "ring" can consist of up to 32 connected MAUs or a maximum of 256 nodes.

Token passing. The second defining characteristic of token ring is the protocol by which it allows shared transmission access to the cable. In a token ring network a single electronic "token" is

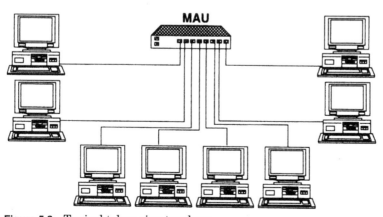

Figure 5.3   Typical token ring topology.

passed around the ring from node to node. If the token is "free" when it reaches a node, that node can attach a message to it, set it to "busy," and pass it along to the next node. The token is then passed from node to node until it gets to the node for which the message is intended. That node reads the message and passes the token along, still busy. When the token returns to the sender and message receipt is verified, the original sender sets the token to "free" and passes it along. Theoretically, with limits on how long any one node can hold a token "busy" and known number of nodes (hence the 256-node limit), it is possible to calculate exactly how long the maximum length of time could be before any given node would be allowed access. A token ring network is thus characterized as "deterministic" as opposed to Ethernet's "probabilistic" nature.

Conclusion

Each of these networks offers its own strengths and weaknesses. Components of an Ethernet network, as the more mature, have almost achieved commodity status and thus are very inexpensive. Basic Ethernet network adapter cards cost between $150 and $350. The interoperability of the components provided by the many different vendors is assured and their reliability very high.

Token ring has the distinction of IBM's blessing and is the primary method by which IBM's mainframes and AS/400 connect to local area networks. Although much is made, by token ring adherents, of the 16-Mbit/s token ring's greater potential throughput and the superiority of a deterministic approach to media access, the impact of these advantages under normal operating conditions is insignificant. Because of its relative youth and lack of widespread support, the cost of token ring components tends to be higher than their Ethernet equivalents. For example, the typical 4/16-Mbit/s token ring adapter card will cost three to four times that of an equivalent Ethernet adapter.

The OSI Model

Any discussion of components that go into making up a network, whether Ethernet or token ring, should begin with a basic overview of the International Standards Organization's (ISO) Open Systems Interconnect (OSI) model. Prior to the OSI model, and to a major extent today, computer networks were based on proprietary technologies unique to specific OEMs. Examples of the most widely used models include IBM's Systems Network Architecture (SNA) and Digital Equipment's DEC Network Architecture (DNA, also known as *DECNet*). These architectures defined the types of communication hardware, lines, and protocols that could be used to allow intelligible communication between computers and other devices available from those vendors. The OSI model grew out of a recognized need to establish a standard, nonproprietary, network architecture that could be a stable foundation on which to build a network that would interconnect proprietary computers from many different OEM sources. Although adherence to the OSI model is not yet widespread, this model still provides an excellent framework within which to discuss networking.

The concept of a protocol is one that is central to data communications across a network. A protocol, in the context of computer communication, can be best thought of as simply a set of rules that hardware and software components use to describe and govern the valid types of messages that can be sent between two parties. The key elements of a protocol are its syntax, semantics, and, for electrical signal protocols, timing specifications. The syntax of a protocol essentially describes the standard format of a message. Protocol syntax describes the allowable contents of the message in terms of how it is structured. Timing, a set of rules primarily associated with electronic signals, defines the mechanisms by which messages that may travel at different speeds and arrive in a different order than they were sent can be sorted out and processed. As we discuss the OSI model and review the various networking components, you should keep in mind that these technologies are implemented as real products and don't always exactly match the OSI model.

As illustrated in Fig. 5.4, the OSI model is a partitioning of a system's functions into seven distinct layers. Each layer describes one aspect of the system environment and the protocols that govern that layer's interaction with the layers directly above and below it.

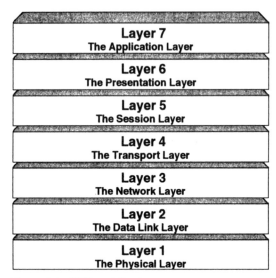

Figure 5.4 OSI architecture.

Layer 1: the physical layer

The physical layer of the OSI model deals with the hardware required to provide a connection between two devices. The components most often thought of as residing at the physical layer are the cabling through which the signal moves, repeaters that are sometimes used to extend the allowable distance between two nodes, any intercable connections such as patch panels or punchdown blocks that may be used, and, in some cases, any centralized concentrators or hubs used to establish star configurations.

Layer 2: the data-link layer

Once a physical connection is established, the signals through that connection need to be interpreted, generated, and controlled in accordance with a set of protocols. At this level of the model these protocols are primarily electrical in nature and implemented in hardware assisted by software to move the data represented by the signal from the wire to computer memory where it can be further processed. In a local area network the network adapter card and the network adapter card driver are the primary examples of components at the data-link layer.

Layer 3: the network layer

The network layer is concerned primarily with determining the physical routing of information across the network and is of particular importance in wide area networks where intelligent routing of packets between nodes that may be accessible from many different paths is very important. This layer normally does not play a significant part in typical local area network as all the node addresses are "local" and generally accessible from only a single path.

Layer 4: the transport layer

The transport layer performs the addressing and routing functions for nodes that are "local" to the network. The purpose of this layer is the packaging and logical addressing of outgoing information and the unpackaging and reading of the contents of arriving packets. It is at this layer that the various types of LAN protocols and network operating systems begin to manifest their own uniqueness. Novell's Netware, for example, uses IPX to implement this layer, while Unix systems generally base their communication on TCP/IP. It is at layer 4 and above that today's LAN protocols and components begin to diverge from the OSI model, combining many of the functions of layers 4, 5, and sometimes 6 into a single protocol or particular piece of software. The term "protocol stack" is often used to describe components such as IPX, NetBios, and TCP/IP that reside at this layer.

Layer 5: the session control layer

This layer is responsible for implementing the protocols that allow two programs to establish and control a session of communication. A session can be thought of as a group of transactions or a logical unit of work that can be marked by a beginning, n transactions of a specific type (security, administration, data request, remote program execution, etc.), and an end. The functions this layer performs are critically important to client/server computing and are often embedded, along with transport layer functions, into the same software. Novell's session control protocol, SPX, is implemented along with IPX in the same software, while Microsoft's Named Pipes and the server message block (SMB) protocol used by NetBios perform functions at this level.

Layer 6: the presentation layer

The top two layers of the OSI model deal less with networking functions, as I think of them, but with operating system and application interfaces, and, in my opinion, the higher you go in the OSI model, the fuzzier the distinctions get between what function goes into what layer.

The OSI presentation layer is responsible for providing the interfaces between the application and the various services and resources required by that application. The difficulty lies in defining "application." For example, the OSI model would characterize certain parts of operating systems, GUIs, and database management software as "applications" in the same sense that an order entry system or word-processing software are applications. This makes the boundary between layers 6 and 7 somewhat indistinct, leaving only such low-level functions as the basic input/output system (BIOS), video drivers, and disk drivers as clearly layer 6 functions. Arguments could be made for components such as Microsoft's MAPI (mail application programming interface), GUI APIs, the X-Window's protocols, Unix's "sockets," and possibly database access APIs for categorization as residing in either layer 6 or layer 7.

Layer 7: the application layer

The top layer is the application itself or that portion with which the user interacts directly. As stated above, the OSI definition of an application is somewhat broad and includes the operating system, GUI, the database management software, and, in the more traditional sense of the term, the actual applications themselves.

Reality

Now that you have an understanding of the accepted "standard" model of a system's perspective, what are the components and technologies that make up the networking portion of the client/server foundation? Referring back to the client/server model illustrated in Fig. 3.2, the network foundation serves as the connection between the application, in the more traditional "order entry system" sense of the term, and the database engine in which the application stores and manipulates its data (see also Fig. 5.5).

Node components

These are the network components that are installed on both the client and server nodes that provide physical connection to the network, apply the appropriate protocols to govern normal network specific communication between all layers, and, in the case of a database server, provide the network-specific layer that allows the database access functions to communicate with the appropriate network protocols.

DB-net interface.   With most, not necessarily all, database servers the database access functions contain a lower-level layer that isolates the database's data access layer, the call-level function library, from the intricacies of the network-specific transport/session level protocols and that may add additional command and unique session control facilities of its own. Examples of this component include Microsoft's DBMSSPX3.DLL implementing IPX/SPX protocols for SQLServer, Novell's OS/2 requester providing named pipes support for Microsoft's OS/2 SQLServer on Novell networks, and Sybase's series of Netlib facilities that provide support for Sybase's SQLServer operating under a number of different operating systems to be accessed across different transport protocols. Another example of this cat-

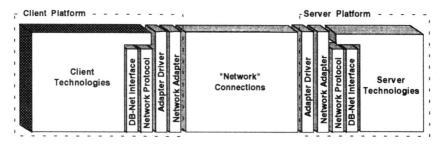

Figure 5.5   Client/server model.

egory is Gupta's SQLRouter, which provides a single development tool or family of tools, in this case Gupta's SQLWindows,
Quest, etc., with access to many different database servers
across many different transport protocols. This class of components exist at level 6 or level 7 of the OSI model.

Network protocol.   The network protocol software in today's
LAN software (for example) is responsible for the OSI level 4
and/or level 5 functions of logically addressing a packet, correctly formatting the information put into the packet, sometimes implementing session control facilities, and passing the
resulting packet directly to the network adapter driver at the
data-link level. This component is also responsible for accepting
the hand-off of incoming packets from the network adapter driver, verifying the format and accuracy of their contents, and
passing the resulting data to either the session layer or directly
to the presentation layer depending on configuration and network. Examples of components that reside at this level include
IPX/SPX, NetBios, and TCP/IP.

Network adapter driver.   The driver is a small piece of software,
generally written by the adapter's manufacturer, that is specific
to the network card and controls its operation and how it moves
data to and from the computer's memory. The major factor in
the performance of a network adapter card is often the efficiency of this driver. For instance, 8- and 16-bit network
adapter cards from one vendor can often outperform superior
32-bit bus mastering cards from other vendors simply on the
basis of more efficient driver software. A de facto standard
method of interfacing with network adapter drivers grew up
over the years and, as the vast majority of LANs traditionally
used a single transport protocol (i.e., IPX/SPX or TCP/IP), this
de facto standard was sufficient to establish interoperability
between various network adapter card vendors and network
operating system products.

   The advent of client/server applications added complexity to
this situation by creating the need for a client platform to
simultaneously connect to various different servers that "spoke"
different transport protocols. One of the alternatives developed
to meet this need is to make it possible for different transport

protocol software to "share" access to the network adapter driver, something that was impossible under the original de facto standard. To facilitate these two different standards for drivers, Microsoft's Network Device Interface Standard (NDIS) and Novell's Open Datalink Interface (ODI) were developed. Drivers written to one or the other (or both) allow those network adapter cards to simultaneously support multiple different protocols through the same card. If you contemplate needing such a capability, then compliance with NDIS, ODI, or both should be a consideration in the selection of network adapters.

Network adapter card. The network adapter card physically connects the client and server to the network medium, accepts, encodes and/or decodes packets, and sends packets on the cable in accordance with the transmission and media access protocols (i.e., Ethernet or token ring) of that network. One of the main functions of the network adapter is to be able to read packet addresses and determine whether the packet is meant for the adapter's node and, if it is, to decode its contents. The ways in which these addresses are specified, the format of the information inside the envelope, and the way the accuracy and completeness of the information are verified is determined by the network's protocol. Network adapter cards are specific to both the network and the type of cabling being used. For example, there are Ethernet coax (coaxial cable), thin coax, and 10BaseT cards.

Two primary hardware characteristics play a role in the performance of a network card, the width of the bus interface and the mechanism used to move data from the card to computer memory. Adapter cards are available in 8-, 16-, and 32-bit versions, and the wider the data path, the faster the card can transfer data to and from the computer itself. The second factor is the method used by the card to pass "data" to the computer itself. Programmed I/O, direct memory access (DMA), shared memory, and bus mastering are various techniques used; shared memory and bus mastering are the fastest and most efficient methods. For client purposes the method used is relatively insignificant as the throughput is rarely high enough to make a noticeable difference one way or another. This is somewhat more important in adapter cards meant for servers. By their nature, servers are shared resources that can normally expect a much higher throughput than can a client with a corresponding greater need for maximum performance.

Network connectivity components

These include the network components that exist external to the client and server platforms and provide the physical connection between the network adapter cards installed on the client and server nodes. In the simplest possible two-node Ethernet network this could be limited to a single piece of wire. In complex networks it can consist of many different components, each providing a different piece of the connectivity puzzle. The most common of the components found in this group are described in the following paragraphs.

Media. The media through which the signal passes are most often a cable that establishes a physical connection between devices on the network. These media are considered to exist at level 1 of the OSI model. The three basic types of cable used are coaxial cable, similar to what you find in your house for cable TV; twisted-pair wiring, similar to that used in telephone installations; and fiber-optic cabling. Each of these types have advantages and disadvantages, differing performance characteristics, and vary widely in cost. Further, there are subtypes of each specially created to meet various operating conditions and requirements.

Coaxial cable. Coax cable consists of a central copper core surrounded by substantial metallic shielding, one or more layers of insulation, and wrapped in a thick plastic or rubber casing. It is supplied in a number of different types that are determined by its design and the materials used in its construction. These types are identified by ratings of the cable's impedance characteristics. These ratings are important because different network cabling schemes require cables with specific characteristics. Coax, in a variety of different ratings, is manufactured in both thick and thin versions, and its primary advantages are its ability to carry a signal for a relatively long distance (1000 to 1500 ft) without needing to have its signal boosted and its resistance to external electromagnetic interference, and it is often used in environments where such interference is extensive. Its primary disadvantage is that it is difficult to install, particularly in small cable runs where room is limited, because of its lack of flexibility and its size.

Twisted-pair cable. Twisted-pair cabling is manufactured in a number of different configurations and exists in both shielded and unshielded versions. Unshielded twisted-pair cable is the least expensive of the cabling options and is rapidly gaining in popularity because of its low cost and the ease with which it can be installed. Unshielded twisted pair is the foundation of most building telephone systems, and it is often possible to utilize unused telephone pairs in newer buildings, although care should be taken to ensure that such pairs are tested and of data-grade quality. Twisted-pair cabling also comes in a variety of different shielded versions that can approach the shielding characteristics of coaxial cable. The primary advantages of twisted-pair cable, in either shielded or unshielded versions, is its low cost and ease of installation. The primary disadvantage is the relatively limited run length (i.e., distance between two points) of 250 to 350 ft and, in unshielded versions, its lack of resistance to external electromagnetic interference.

Fiber-optic cable. Fiber-optic cable is cable where the normal copper wire has been replaced by glass fibers through which light is used to pass signals, not electric current. This is the most expensive of the cabling options in terms of both the cost of the cable itself and, because of the special knowledge and tools needed, its installation cost. A popular misconception is that speed is the primary advantage of fiber-optic cable. In fact, electric signals move through copper practically as fast as light travels through glass fibers. The main advantages of fiber-optic cable are primarily transmission distance and reliability. Fiber-optic cable can easily transmit signals up to 2 mi without boosting. Further, fiber-optic signals cannot be disrupted by external electromagnetic interference.

Repeaters. A repeater is basically a simple protocol independent signal booster that is used wherever a single point-to-point run of cable exceeds the distance rating of the cabling being used. A repeater intercepts the signal, retimes it, and then retransmits the signal as it was when transmitted from its original source. Repeaters are considered OSI level 1 components.

Concentrators. LANs that implement a star topology (token ring, Ethernet 10BaseT, etc.) require one or more semicentralized hubs to which media runs from the nodes. These hubs are variously known as *multistation access units* or *concentrators,* are generally protocol-specific, and provide centralized point-to-point connections for each node to the hub. These hubs can be interconnected with other hubs, allowing the network to grow to its specified maximum number of nodes. These hubs can range from the simple and inexpensive standard passive IBM eight-port token ring MAU to complex, multifunction, rank-mounted concentrators such as the Synoptics 3000 series, which can themselves host multiple MAUs of different protocols in internal expansion slots. In the typical star topology the cabling does not run directly from the node to the concentrator but to an intermediate wire-to-wire component that simplifies maintenance and reconfiguration of network connections. Punchdown blocks, AT&T type 100 wirewrap boards, and RJ-45 patch pannels are examples of the components most often used to provide this wire-to-wire connection. Wire-to-wire components and basic concentrators are essentially OSI level 1 components. Larger, more complex concentrator technologies can, depending on their flexibility, exist and host other components that exist throughout levels 1, 2, and 3 of the OSI model.

Bridge. A bridge is a hardware component that serves to connect two separate networks, passing packets across from one to the other only when the packet is addressed to a node on the other network. Only one bridge is required to interconnect two physically adjacent networks, but two bridges are required when the networks are separated by distances greater than the node-to-node restrictions applicable to the network. Bridges are often used to physically segment large local area networks into smaller segments in order to control throughput volume, increase performance, link two networks using different types of cabling, or link two networks using different MAC protocols (i.e., token ring to Ethernet). Bridges maintain addresses of the nodes on each side of the bridge and only pass packets from one side that are addressed to the other. Bridges operate at the data link layer or level 2 of the OSI model.

Router and brouter.   A router is a hardware component that is similar to a bridge but which is generally used to serve wider geographic areas and serve to link any two points by encoding special routing instructions that can be used by the third network that serves to connect the two separate routers to intelligently select different paths for the transmission. Routers can server to interconnect networks that use completely different MAC and transport layer protocols. Routers do not maintain node addresses for the interconnected networks and must be addressed specifically by the nodes or other routers seeking transmission of their packets. The functions of the router place it at level 3 of the OSI model.

A brouter is a hardware component that combines the functions of bridges and routers.

Gateway.   Consisting of both hardware and software, this component allows a network to be "attached" to another significantly different network using different MAC and transport protocols. From the perspective of the "external" network, the gateway appears as a device standard to that network. Novell's Netware SNA is an example of a commonly found gateway. It consists of hardware (expansion card) that connects to an IBM SNA network and software that makes that gateway "look like" a 327x terminal control unit to the mainframe and devices on that network "look like" attached 3279 terminal devices.

6

Server
Technologies

The server functions as the shared resource half of the client/server equation. As such it must be able to service multiple, often simultaneous, requests for data from the various application clients throughout the network. The technology of the server platform can range from basically equivalent to the client up to and including large mainframes. This server flexibility is the foundation of client/server architecture's scalability. As one of the two primary shared resources of the architecture (cable bandwidth is the other), the server provides the processor cycles, data storage subsystems, memory, and bus bandwidth shared by hundreds of clients, and relatively minor upgrades to the server's capacity can have immediate and disproportionately beneficial effects on the perceived performance of the client application.

The downside of this characteristic is that, just like any multiuser mainframe system, its failure drops not just a single user of the application but all the users of all the applications depending on it for service. Thus, the driving factors in selection and configuration of server technologies are stability first, performance second, and flexibility third. While it is rarely advantageous to base client platforms on proprietary technologies, proprietary technologies can often provide substantial benefits in stability and performance, provided connectivity can be established.

Another factor to consider in the selection and configuration of the server technology is to determine what functions it will perform. For example, it is quite possible to set up and operate a client/server environment without a network operating system to manage access to the network's shared resources. Although possible, it is rarely recommended, and if the full value of the network and shared resources are to be realized, a network operating system is essential. But the client/server architecture provides significant flexibility in how that environment, as a whole, is configured. For example, if a network operating system is present, the database services can be based on the same platform as the network operating system, sharing access to processor and data storage with other typical network functions, or the database services can be located on an entirely separate platform dedicated to database services, as illustrated in Fig. 6.1 (see also Fig. 6.2).

A network can have many different servers, all playing different roles, providing the same or different services. The dedicated database server's primary function is to manage and respond to multiple simultaneous requests to the database management software. File servers, generally the "home" of the network operating system, are multipurpose, providing, at a minimum, network security and shared access to files. In addition, file servers, as the home of the network operating system, also often provide for the sharing of network printers, implement communication gateways to the outside world, gather network performance statistics, and provide administration and management functions necessary to enhance the environment's

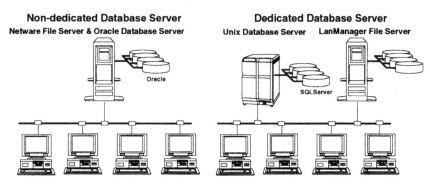

Figure 6.1 Dedicated versus non-dedicated.

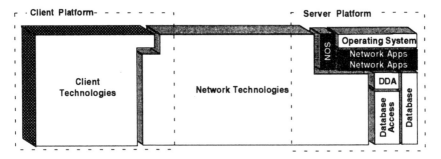

Figure 6.2 Server operating system.

stability. In some situations it can be advantageous to distribute some or all of these services across many different servers, each dedicated to a specific task (print server, communication server, etc.).

Server Operating System

Like the client's operating system, the primary purpose of the server operating system is to provide applications operating on that server with access to the hardware resources (memory, disk data storage, video and printer output, etc.) of that server and manage the interfaces between that workstation and devices external to that workstation (video, printer, etc.). Unlike the client, the nature of the server's mission as a shared resource for many clients requires greater sophistication and functionality beyond that needed by the typical client, and the facilities it provides closely resemble those provided by proprietary multiuser operating systems. For example, the ability to multitask is not an option but a requirement, and preemptive multitasking, providing greater tolerance for program failure, is generally preferable to cooperative multitasking. The ability to directly address large amounts of memory is also a prerequisite, with 16 Mbytes of storage considered a basic minimum to provide basic functionality and the capacity to extend that storage far beyond this a significant advantage.

An operating system that provides administration and management capabilities, access security, shared client access to files, printer queuing and routing, and various other functions is generally referred to as a *network operating system* (NOS) and can take a number of different forms. Some network operating systems are full-function operating systems that have been designed specifically to meet the needs of networked resource sharing. Novell's Netware and Banyan's Vines are examples of this approach. Others, such as Microsoft's LanManager and the network file system (NFS) extensions to Unix, are extensions to multitasking operating systems that add the security, administration and management, routing, and other functions that are specific to networked resource sharing.

Network operating systems also take two different architectural approaches to sharing resources across the network. The peer-to-peer approach blurs the distinction between client and server by essentially making it possible for every network node, running that operating system, to play the role of either client or server. Each such node can be servicing a specific user as a workstation while simultaneously sharing its data storage, processor, or printer resources with the network. Unix is an example of such a peer-to-peer approach, while OS/2 workstations in LanManager networks can play a limited peer-to-peer role. The network server approach requires the dedication of one or more specific platforms as the network operating system's "home," and it is only those platforms whose resources can be shared. Whether peer-to-peer or dedicated, a full-featured operating system or simply an extension, the network operating system should provide, at a minimum, the following functions:

- *Resource sharing*—provide controlled access to the basic shared resources of the network.

- *Administration*—the ability to identify and define the authorized users of the network, the resources those users can access, the locations of those users, and other information that aids in controlling and managing access to network resources.

- *Resource management*—those functions that allow diagnosis and correction of problems on both the network and the server, monitoring of resource utilization, the ability to optimize performance of the server in specific situations, and provision of capacity planning capabilities. This area is one where proprietary approaches often offer vastly superior functionality over the more open operating systems and network operating systems available for industry standard hardware configurations.

- *Fault tolerance*—the ability of a server to recover from the failure of one or more of its components without interrupting service to the network. There are many different levels and types of fault tolerance. At the lowest level of fault tolerance is the operating system's ability to survive the abnormal termination of a program executing within that operating system. Higher levels of fault tolerance can include error-correcting memory, disk mirroring (data written to two disks at same time so that if one breaks, the other takes up the slack automatically), disk duplexing (where an entire disk subsystem including the disk controller is duplexed so that if a controller breaks, the alternative subsystem kicks in automatically), and even server duplexing where an entire duplicate server is standing by being constantly updated so that it takes over instantaneously if the primary server fails. As you might guess, the greater the fault tolerance, the greater the expense. This is another area where proprietary approaches often offer vastly superior functionality. These operating systems and hardware configurations have provided these capabilities for years, while solutions based on industry standard technologies are just beginning to provide the same functionality as "add-ons" to the basic platforms.

Server Hardware

This is the basic server technology foundation on which everything else rests. Server hardware can range from basically equivalent to the client to large proprietary configurations. Unlike the client, the server must be able to provide responsive service to multiple simultaneous client requests while ensuring a stable and secure environment. The disk storage subsystem is possibly the single most important determining factor in a server's performance and reliability. The vast majority of client requests will be for data, and the disk storage subsystem represents the "choke point" through which these requests must pass. Further, as the major "mechanical" moving part in a configuration, the hard disks that make up the disk storage subsystem are the most prone to failure of any component of the platform.

Given these factors, special attention should be directed toward selecting and configuring the disk storage subsystems of any platform expected to perform a significant server role in one or more applications. Storage subsystems are available in a variety of forms, both proprietary and based on industry standards, each offering their own advantages. Suffice it to say, without going into great technical detail, that a server's disk storage subsystem should provide for very high-speed transfer of data from disk drive to system memory, multiple concurrent paths to and from data so that requests are not single-threaded, and some form of seek optimization so that "data" can be located efficiently and quickly.

Database Access

This component can either stand alone as an easily recognized module or be embedded in the architecture of the database management system itself, but, in either case, it is specific to the database management software being used and functions essentially as a request manager. This component serves to isolate the database engine itself from the network protocols being used, manages the client connection to the database engine, translates and transmits the client request to the engine, accepts and sometimes buffers the request result, and interacts with the network protocol to transmit those results back to the client.

This component is often a controlling factor in a database engine's resource usage and sometimes serves to constrain how many clients may be supported simultaneously. For example, early versions of Oracle for the OS/2 platform required 256K (256 kbytes of memory) or more for each client connection due to Oracle's internal architecture. Although this architecture enhanced performance for a limited number of clients, it served as a significant limit to the total number of simultaneous connections that could be supported in OS/2 1.x's 16-Mbyte address space. In comparison, SQLServer's internal architecture made effective use of OS/2 threads and reentrancy to reduce resource per connection requirements to less than 60K, therefore trading off some individual client performance under lightly loaded conditions to the ability to adequately support a far larger number of simultaneous connections.

Distributed Data Access

This function may or may not be present depending on the database software being used. When present, it will be specific to the database management software and may be provided as a standard facility or as an extra cost option. The purpose of this component, where it is present, is to facilitate and manage communication between two or more database servers residing on similar or different platforms across the network. This communication most generally takes the form of requests for data or updates to data that are "remote" from the server making the requests. For example, Fig. 6.3 illustrates a client communicating a request to database server 1. Database server 1 does not have that data available locally but knows where it is and "forwards" the request to the remote server 2, who then responds. Database server 1 then returns the data to the client.

Another variation on this can be distributed data update where an update to data residing on server 1 triggers updates to data residing on one or more remote servers. In this more complex example, the distributed data access function must provide the capability, usually referred to as "two-phase commit," of ensuring that all updates are successfully completed before either committing those updates or canceling them. The functionality and capability of this component will be dependent on the database vendor and its actual usefulness and importance determined by the business's requirements.

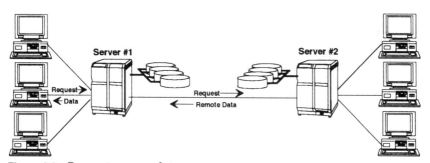

Figure 6.3 Server to server data access.

Proprietary extensions to support remote data distribution
have traditionally been offered by various database vendors
and serve to support, more or less, many of these data access
needs. Oracle and INGRES, in particular, have long incorporated some form of distributed data access capability within
their products. The problem to date, though, has been to provide such access across heterogeneous database platforms.

IBM, as the only vendor providing multiple different and
incompatible SQL database products today, has published a
Distributed Relational Data Architecture (DRDA) specification
that offers one potential solution to this problem. Currently
implemented in IBM's various platform specific Distributed
Database Connection Service (DRDS) products to provide
transparent distributed access to DB/2, SQL/400, SQL/DS, and
OS/2 Data Manager, IBM has offered this specification to the
SQL access group as a basis for an industry-wide distributed
processing standard.

A third approach to this problem is represented by Sybase's
Open Data Services product. Open Data Services is essentially
an API supported by a function library that facilitates the
building of database specific gateways between SQLServer and
other database products in a manner that is transparent to the
application itself. The ODS layer resides on the server and
monitors all client requests, intercepting and rerouting those
meant for other database servers, then passing the remote
database's response back to the requester as if it had been ser-
viced locally. Although this is a very flexible and powerful solution to a number of specific "problems," the "roll your own" distribution mechanism isn't appropriate for most application
developers and its use is limited to third-party middleware vendors developing such database specific gateways as
MicroDecisionWare's DB/2 gateway.

Database Engine

The last—and most important from the developer's point of
view—component of the server is the database engine itself.
The database engine is a server application configured specifically to manage the storage, retrieval, update, and manipulation of data. Unlike typical personal computer databases, where

all database functions are executed on the personal computer, the client/server database puts all the data selection, sorting, updating, indexing, and other data manipulation functions at the server. Because of the importance of this component in the client/server architecture and the complexity of today's typical relational database engines, I will cover this topic in more detail in Chap. 8.

Now that we have an understanding of the basic technologies and components used as the foundation for client/server architectures, the next chapter will put these technologies in perspective by illustrating how these components are used in putting together actual client/server configurations.

7

Configurations

The client/server approach's flexibility is both one of its greatest strengths and the source of the majority of technical problems usually experienced in client/server development. In the previous chapters we discussed the well-defined and clearly delineated functional layers on which the client/server environment is based. Unfortunately, in the real world, actual implementation of these functions is rarely so well defined, and it is at this level that the greatest problems are encountered by the developer attempting to integrate all the pieces in order to establish a stable foundation.

The ways in which these various layers are implemented vary widely from vendor to vendor, and any given configuration will tend to be unique to a specific environment. This chapter will illustrate this complexity by reviewing a number of typical client/server configurations for different client and server platforms, network operating systems, transport protocols, and database management systems. As you review these, you will no doubt notice that MS-DOS/Windows clients are the most often used example. The reasons for this are that (1) Windows is currently the most popular and least expensive of the GUI workstation alternatives for client/server configurations; (2) because of some of the unique limitations and workarounds associated with MS-Windows, it is often one of the more difficult clients to configure in a client/server environment; and (3) it is the alternative I am personally most familiar with. DOS/Windows is not necessarily the "best" client platform in many environments, and other client solutions, most notably the Macintosh System 7 and several inexpensive Unix workstations, can often offer equal or superior functionality. Further, please keep in mind as you review these configurations that they are only a few of the options available and, for any given combination of transport protocol, operating systems, and database management systems, there can be a number of variations in individual components and even in configuration alternatives.

Sybase SQLServer Unix-to-Unix Configuration

Unix-to-Unix platforms were the first to host a client/server architecture, as the term has come to be known today. As the progenitor of today's proliferation of client/server environments, Unix is still the simplest of the configurations to implement even when the client and server platforms are operating with different flavors of Unix on proprietary or semiproprietary hardware. This simplicity is due, in large extent, to the standardization of TCP/IP as the transport protocol. The various implementations of TCP/IP sockets, through which the software interacts with the underlying TCP/IP protocol stack, are often vendor or third-party software, and integration problems can sometimes arise. But this is a minor issue, compared with the problems that occur in more heterogeneous environments, and is easily resolved by following OEM and database vendor configuration recommendations. Figure 7.1 illustrates a typical Unix-to-Unix client/server configuration using Sybase's SQLServer.

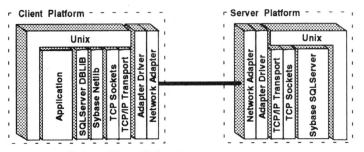

Figure 7.1   Unix to Unix (Sybase).

DBLIB—the call-level interface provides the function library to which the application writes its requests and from which the application receives the database's result set.

Sybase Netlib—functions as the interface between the DB-Library functions and the transport layer TCP/IP protocol stack. In Sybase's case the Netlib is specific to a particular TCP/IP socket or transport layer interface (TLI) implementation within that specific client's Unix environment.

TCP/IP sockets—the high-level software interface to the actual TCP/IP protocol stack. Socket implementations often tend to have minor differences between various OEM and third-party software providers and can often be a source of integration problems.

Adapter driver/adapter—MAC layer driver and physical connection to the network media.

Sybase SQLServer—database software providing the server functionality. As SQLServer software is specific to the Unix environment for which it is configured, it communicates directly with the standard TCP/IP sockets for that environment.

MS-Windows to OS/2 SQLServer

Using industry standard software and hardware, this configuration is primarily responsible for popularizing the concept of client/server architectures in non-Unix environments. Because of its relatively low cost of entry, this configuration provided opportunities to deploy client/server applications to smaller groups of users more cost-effectively than typical Unix-to-Unix implementations. Although this configuration was initially limited to Microsoft LanManager environments, there are now a number of different possible configurations.

LanManager

The "standard" MS-Windows-to-OS/2 SQLServer configuration uses the named pipes interprocess communication protocol that is a part of the LanManager network operating system and would be configured as illustrated in Fig. 7.2.

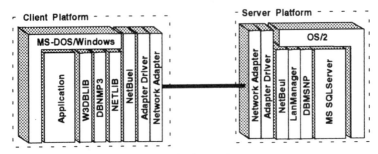

Figure 7.2   Windows to OS/2 (SQLServer).

W3DBLIB—the call-level interface which provides the function library to which the application writes its requests and from which the application receives the database's result set.

DBNMP3—maps the output of the W3DBLIB calls to named pipes command formats and passes commands to NETLIB.

NETLIB—maps the protected-mode named pipes calls to real-mode transfer to NetBeui transport protocol.

NetBeui—LanManager transport layer protocol (i.e., equivalent to NetBios functions).

Adapter driver/adapter—MAC layer driver and physical connection to the network media.

DBMNP—named pipes command interface between the network and SQLServer.

Novell Netware with Named Pipes

A MS-Windows to OS/2 SQLServer can also operate in a Novell Netware network operating system environment. Two different alternatives are available to support this alternative. The first continues to use named pipes as the command protocol and transports named pipes packets using several Novell supplied alternatives, as illustrated in Fig. 7.3.

DOSNP—provided by Novell; traps the hand-off of real-mode named pipes calls, prepares the calls for IPX, and passes control to IPXSPX.

IPX/SPX—Novell Netware transport layer protocol.

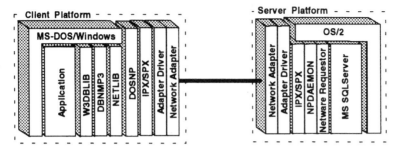

Figure 7.3 Windows to OS/2 (SQLServer) over Netware using named pipes.

Adapter driver / adapter—MAC layer driver and physical connection to the network media.

NPDAEMON—works with Netware IPX/SPX to provide the transport layer with NetBeui-equivalent named pipes functions.

Netware OS / 2 requester—extends Netware to add named pipes interface to OS/2 and OS/2 applications (i.e., the database).

Novell Netware without Named Pipes

A MS-Windows to OS/2 SQLServer connection can also be operated in a Novell Netware environment using standard Netware transport without named pipes support. This capability is provided through Microsoft's Network Integration Kit. Given the history of instability associated with Novell's OS/2 requester and its limitations, this is advantageous in several ways. The first, and possibly most important, is that it works reliably. The second advantage is that it decreases the number of layers through which requests and results are passed, making more memory available on the client side and increasing the performance of the client/server connection. There is no such thing as a free lunch, though, and this third alternative has several limitations which, for most clients, will have little impact. A number of SQLServer database administration products (software that facilitates the setup, administration, and management of SQLServer) require named pipes to transport specific commands. These tools will not work with Microsoft's Netware Network Integration Kit. Another limitation concerns the use of SQLServer's Open Data Services

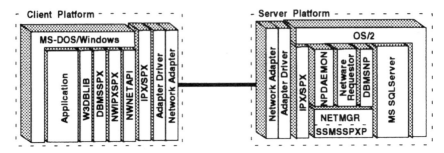

Figure 7.4 Windows to OS/2 (SQLServer) over Netware using IPX/SPX.

(ODS) facilities, which are also dependent on named pipes (see section on using gateways to establish connectivity). As the OS/2 server can provide simultaneous named pipes (still through Novell's OS/2 requester) and native IPX/SPX, these limitations can be overcome by having database administrators and ODS clients continue to use DOSNP and the OS/2 requester while normal clients can switch to native IPX/SPX protocols. Figure 7.4 illustrates this configuration.

DBMSSPX3—provides the high-level network interface functionality previously supplied by DBNMPIPE, taking the requests from W3DBLIB which, by the way, is specific to this alternative.

NWIPXSPX—works with DBMSSPX3 to package the requests for transfer to transport-level IPX/SPX.

NWNETAPI—maps the protected mode IPX/SPX calls to real-mode transfer to IPX/SPX transport protocol.

SSMSSPXP—functions as the server's network library for normal IPX/SPX interface.

Network manager—acts as the manager of communication between the network library and SQLServer or SQLServer's ODS functions; logs onto the network and registers the server in the appropriate Netware Bindery as a network service.

MS-Windows to Oracle v7.0 Unix

The Oracle database management system, as one of the first commercial relational products, offers a popular and mature database technology. Oracle's SQL*NET technology provides a richly functional, network transparent distributed database access across multiple Oracle servers operating in different environments. In addition to its distributed database functionality, the SQL*NET line of products are Oracle's approach to isolating both the client and the server from dependence on any given network transport protocol. Oracle's GLUE facility is a database-independent (initially limited to Oracle databases) call-level interface, introduced in mid-1993, which serves as their application interface to SQL*NET. Figure 7.5 illustrates a typical MS-Windows-to-Oracle Unix configuration.

appGLUE—an application call-level interface to Oracle server databases. This call-level interface is available in either a generic form or application-specific forms that provide greater integration with such specific tools as Visual Basic and Microsoft's Excel.

SQLGLUE—the portion of the GLUE facility that provides the mapping of SQL statements across database management software from multiple vendors, although initially limited to Oracle databases.

GLUE—a module containing functions used by other modules within the GLUE product and providing, among other functions, the hand-off of properly formatted SQL statements to SQL*NET for transmissions to the appropriate server.

*SQL*NET*—the high-level software interface to the network. SQL*NET also plays an extended role in the transparent intelligent routing of client requests to the appropriate database server by establishing a database of all available database servers, with their network and location uniquely identi-

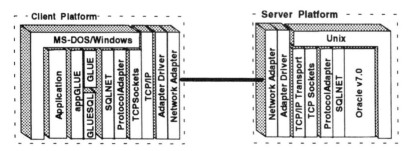

Figure 7.5 Windows to Unix (Oracle).

fied by an alias that is addressed by a client application as if the database were local.

Protocol adapters—the low-level software that matches SQL*NET's high-level network interface to a specific protocol and, in the case of TCP/IP, to specific sockets or TLI implementation. The protocol adapter makes a given SQL*NET implementation specific to one specific protocol stack and does not support multiple concurrent client or server protocol stacks. Such multiprotocol support for routing purposes is handled through a companion product, Multi-protocol Interchange (proprietary to Oracle), which is a separate software and hardware solution acting almost like a network router to repackage network packages and direct them to the appropriate database server.

TCP/IP sockets—the high-level software interface to the actual TCP/IP protocol stack. Socket implementations often tend to have minor differences between various OEM and third-party software providers and Oracle's protocol adapters are specific to individual socket or TLI implementations.

Adapter driver/adapter—MAC layer driver and physical connection to the network media.

Using Dynamic Data Exchange

Although one of the features of client/server architecture is its freedom from proprietary technologies, this does not mean that proprietary technologies are excluded from the client/server approach. In many situations a proprietary technology can often offer significant advantages, especially as a server platform. Unfortunately, the primary obstacle faced in using such a platform as a server is connectivity. As a proprietary technology, the connectivity alternatives available to such platforms often are very restricted or support only protocols that are unsuitable for client/server communication. In situations such as these the only alternative can often be to link special-purpose connectivity programs with the application through some form of dynamic data exchange.

The AS/400 is an example of such proprietary technology. The AS/400, besides being an immensely popular platform, represents the closest any general-purpose computer has come to being a dedicated database platform. The AS/400's proprietary operating system incorporates a highly functional relational database engine, and, in effect, the operating system is the database or vice versa. With a contiguously addressable memory space measured in the terabytes, the AS/400 DASD is essentially memory-mapped to the operating system and provides extremely efficient data throughput. Combine these attributes with scalability from small 20-user systems to those capable of supporting over a thousand simultaneous multiuser connections, and the AS/400 can be viewed as an almost ideal server platform. The basic obstacle to the AS/400 fulfilling this role is client connectivity, as Figs. 7.6 and 7.7 illustrate.

MS-Windows DDE to AS/400.   Connecting a Windows client to an AS/400 is an example of this use of dynamic data exchange (DDE) to establish a client/server linkage. It uses a set of client resident software to provide a DDE interface to the client appli-

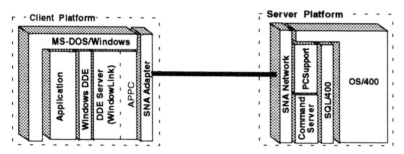

Figure 7.6   Windows DDE to AS/400.

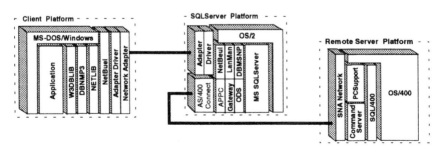

Figure 7.7   Server gateways.

cation, set up and map SQL calls placed through that DDE link to the AS/400, formulate the appropriate advanced program-to-program protocols, and pass those protocols through the client's connection to the AS/400. Connections generally supported include both typical SNA/SDLC links and any local area network implemented on both the client and AS/400. The WindowLink product from Rochester Software Connection, Inc. is an example of this type of configuration. This software "serves" the application's DDE calls, transforming the SQL commands passed to APPC formats, initiating the APPC connection with AS/400, processing the results, and passing them back to the application.

Windows DDE. This is a standard Windows DDE facility through which the application passes SQL commands to WindowLink and through which WindowLink passes the result set. As a transport medium, DDE leaves a great deal to be desired. It requires significant overhead in terms of memory and cycles, has limitations in terms of the amount of data that can be passed, is not a standard method for an application to communicate with a database server, is slow, and, in my opinion, is not sufficiently reliable for production use.

SNA adapter. This is whatever SNA network connection is used to connect the client to the AS/400. It can range from direct twin axial up to and including a full local area network connection using a LAN operating system that provides AS/400 connectivity (Netware for SNA, LanManager's Communication Manager, etc.).

Command server. This approach can be implemented on the AS/400 in several different ways. To support the data transfer and APPC connectivity, the configuration can use IBM's PC Support Services product(s) for the AS/400, or, in some situations, the functionality is implemented using third-party command processing software to provide more efficient linkage to the AS/400's database.

SQL/400. This IBM AS/400 product provides an SQL language interface to the AS/400's native file system–database management system.

Using Gateways to Establish Connectivity

Sometimes there simply is no acceptable or reliable method of establishing direct connectivity between a client and a database to which the client needs access. In other instances there is a business need to enhance an existing client/server database application by providing transparent "pass-through" of SQL requests from the normal database server to another remote data source that would normally be directly inaccessible to the client. This need can often be met by using the normal database server itself as a "gateway" to the remote data sources. In this type of configuration the client portion of the application is blind to where the data is actually coming from while the database server provides the mapping of SQL requests from one dialect to another and provides the connection to the remote data source. Figure 7.6 illustrates this approach, again using a Windows client to access AS/400 data through the mediation of the OS/2 SQLServer's ODS facility.

DBLIB—the call-level interface which provides the function library to which the application writes its requests and from which the application receives the database's result set.

DBNMP3—maps the output of the W3DBLIB calls to named pipes command formats and passes commands to NETLIB.

NETLIB—maps the protected-mode named pipes calls to real-mode transfer to NetBeui transport protocol.

NetBeui—LanManager transport layer protocol (i.e., equivalent to NetBios functions).

Adapter driver/adapter—MAC layer driver and physical connection to the network media.

DBMNP—named pipes command interface between the network and SQLServer.

ODS—the Open Data Services library provided by Sybase. This can be thought of as connection mediator for the SQLServer database engine that, when present, handles all network communications for SQLServer and additionally has an application programming interface so that applications written on the server platform can be initiated and trap and manage client requests to SQLServer, either passing them through to the local SQLServer engine or manipulating them and then rerouting them to other destinations. Results coming back from either the local SQLServer engine or the remote destinations are then handled by the ODS application and returned to the client. In all cases, the processing performed is transparent to the client, and results appear to be returned directly by SQLServer.

Gateway—an application that uses the Open Data Services API to process all client requests and either passes them through to SQLServer or, in this configuration, remaps the request's Sybase SQL to AS/400 SQL, reformats the requests from named pipes to APPC, establishes the APPC linkage with the AS/400 through an SNA connection, and transmits the reformatted request to the AS/400. The results of the request are returned from the AS/400, reformatted as SQLServer results, and returned to the client through the standard named pipes path as if the data had come directly from the local SQLServer engine. A commercially available example of this approach is the ShowCase Gateway product from Rochester Software Connection, Inc.

APPC/communication manager—the facility through which multiple simultaneous connections with both local area network and SNA networks is managed and also provides the necessary APPC facilities for the gateway's use. Examples of communication managers for OS/2 include IBM's Communication Manager and Microsoft/DCA's Communication Server.

SNA connection—provides the physical connection between the gateway server and the AS/400 and can be implemented in any manner consistent with APPC usage that is supported by the AS/400.

Using ODBC and APPC

A far more efficient and effective method of incorporating the AS/400 into a client/server architecture is through the use of an ODBC driver in combination with IBM's standard APPC interprocess protocol. AS/400-specific ODBC drivers, such as those that are just now becoming available, and their use in the

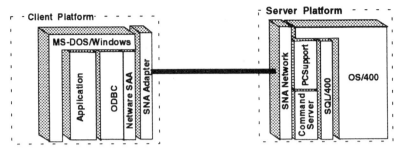

Figure 7.8   ODBC.

AS/400 environment provide a standard, straightforward and efficient connection that overcomes the disadvantage of both the gateway and DDE approaches. Further, because ODBC is based on an emerging standard, this alternative serves to better insulate the application itself from both the AS/400 and APPC. Figure 7.8 illustrates this approach, again using a Windows client to access AS/400 data through an ODBC driver connecting directly to the AS/400 using Novell's Netware SAA APPC driver.

> *ODBC driver*—third-party ODBC driver configured for the AS/400 to implement SQL and data mapping and APPC commands.
>
> *Netware SAA*—MA Novell APPC TSR driver that implements the same functionality as IBM's PC Services Router while requiring far less memory (10K vs. 70K).

Summary

As you can see, there are many alternative configurations that can be used in any given situation to establish a client/server environment. Some are better than others, some are more complex, but the configuration used should be driven by environmental factors and business needs and must work reliably and provide acceptable levels of performance. What is often perceived as client/server complexity is the integration of these configurations, and this integration is the primary source of the technical obstacles associated with establishing and maintaining a client/server environment.

8

The Database Engine

Database engines have existed as commercial products for 20 or more years and have taken a number of different forms, most proprietary, over that time. Early database management software tended to be provided by OEMs seeking to enhance the value of their hardware offerings and tie their customer accounts ever more closely to the vendor. These early database management programs ranged from basic access management oriented indexing (ISAM, VSAM, B-Trees, etc.) to full database management software capable of sophisticated data manipulation (IBM's IMS/DB, Cullinet's IDMS, etc.). The various full-fledged database management packages followed either a hierarchical, networked, or inverted-list model and were each highly proprietary and generally incompatible.

During the 1970s the Data Base Task Group (DBTG) of the Conference on Data Systems Languages (CODASYL), the group responsible at that time for the standardization of the COBOL programming language, attempted to establish a standard specification for a common data query and manipulation language to serve as a model for database management systems. This resulted in what came to be known as the *CODASYL* specification of the network model. Network is used in this sense as a description of the data-set interrelationships, not in terms of communication networks. Although several commercial products, most notably Cincom's TOTAL and Cullinet's IDMS, successfully implemented database management products that were more or less in compliance with these specifications, this early attempt at data language standardization failed to be widely adopted.

The Relational Model

In 1970 Dr. E. F. Codd, an IBM research scientist, published a paper formulating a theory of data manipulation based on the principles of set theory and what was termed "relational algebra." As this was the first attempt to base a data manipulation language on a "provable" mathematical model, it generated significant interest in the industry. Additional work followed until the mid-1970s when researchers from IBM's San Jose (Calif.) Research Laboratory developed an early version of a data manipulation language based on Codd's work. This early precursor of today's SQL was called SEQUEL and formed the basis for an experimental IBM database management system called System R.

While IBM was experimenting with the theories a number of third-party software companies recognized the potential that was represented by a data manipulation language that was grounded in mathematical principles, semiendorsed by IBM, and, best of all, was essentially in the public domain. The first of these to bring commercial database management products to market was Relational Software, Inc, now known as the *Oracle* Corporation, followed closely by Relational Technologies, Inc.'s INGRES database product. Almost from the beginning these companies realized the importance of providing software that was portable across different operating systems and proprietary hardware which, at a time when almost all database products were specific to a given proprietary platform, was a revolutionary approach to portability. Further, thanks to the explicitness of E. F. Codd's Relational Rules, and the ongoing work in relational theory of both E. F. Codd and C. J. Date the various relational database vendors have had a theoretical framework against which to measure their adherence to the relational model. Although few, if any, currently available relational database products fully comply with all of these rules, most are in fundamental compliance.

Additional third-party software providers followed Oracle Corporation and Relational Technologies, Inc.'s lead in bringing SQL-based relational database products to market until today we have a wealth of alternatives from which to choose. Although the various dialects of SQL have varied from vendor to vendor as each has added its own extensions to the language, the core set of SQL that we have today is highly standard and specifications for its implementation governed by the ANSI SQL Committee. Because of the efforts of this committee and vendor recognition of the marketing importance of complying with at least the "core" standards set down in ANSI SQL I and II, SQL has become the lingua franca of the relational database world. As such it is one of the primary factors in the explosion of client/server development activity.

Given the importance of relational database technology and SQL to the development of client/server database applications, the rest of this chapter will provide an overview of the relational database model, the basic capabilities of SQL, the type of extensions to SQL found in typical relational database products, and some of the more important characteristics that should be considering when evaluating relational database management software.

Tables

In a relational database all data is represented as being stored in two-dimensional tables. In the first, horizontal dimension of the rows of the table represent instances of the entity; in the second, vertical dimension each column equates to an attribute of the entity. Each table represents an entity about which you wish to store data. This entity has certain characteristics which serve to describe it. These characteristics are generally referred to as "attributes" and exist as a result of a functional dependence between a single instance of the entity represented by the table and single instances of each attribute value which describe that entity. For example, Fig. 8.1 illustrates a situation where information about two types of entities, "person" and "company," are being tracked. The attributes tracked for person include name, social security number, phone number, street, city, state, zip code, and employer. The attributes for company

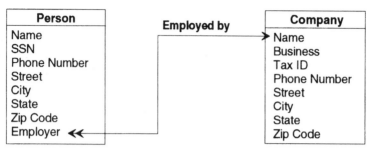

Figure 8.1 Relational tables.

include name, business, tax ID, phone number, street, city, state, and zip code.

The line between the "person" attribute "employer" and the "company" attribute "name" introduces the third element of a relational database, the relationship. In this example, this line indicates that there is a potential relationship between a person and a company called "employed by" and that this relationship is declared by a match between the value of the attribute "employer," for any specific instance of a person, and the value of the attribute "name" for any given instance of a company. In this particular instance we say that the attribute employer, because it is equivalent to an attribute of another entity type, is a foreign key, and we can infer from this that the nature of the relationship is one to many, or one company can have many employees.

These three constructs, "rows," "columns," and "relationships," form the mathematical basis for the power and simplicity of the relational model and the SQL commands that can manipulate that model. Entities equate to tables with individual instances of an entity being a row. Rows are made up of columns that equate to the attributes that are to be stored for all rows of that table. Using only these constructs, or variations on these constructs, the relational theory can encompass designs that accurately model the vast majority of real-world information requirements. Given the model in Fig. 8.1 let us imagine that in the real world we know that a person can work for many companies, not just one. Further, we might like to store more detailed information about those employment relationships. This need introduces a somewhat more complex type of relationship and a special type of entity. As illustrated in Fig. 8.2, the simple one-to-many relationship of Fig. 8.1 has become a many-to-many relationship. Further, because we need to store information (employee, company, title, start, and end) that more fully describes the relationship, it has acquired characteristics of its own. These characteristics transform the simple relationship into a special type of entity that is said to be "functionally dependent" on each of the other entity types to which it is related.

There are a number of variations on these constructs, which I'll cover in more detail in Chap. 13, but these three things, "entities," "attributes," and "relationships," form the foundation of the relational model. Based on this basic mathematical simplicity it was possible to develop a concise and powerful data access and query language to manipulate data structured in this manner. Relational databases all have three basic manipulation principles in common; you are allowed to select (1) one or more of the table's attributes without having to select all of the attributes, (2) one or more of the rows of a table without having to select all of the rows, and (3) from one or more tables at a time.

The relational model is manipulated by four basic operations: "selection," "projection," "join," and "concatenation." Each of these operations can be thought of as returning, in answer to a request, another table that "holds" the results of the operation. This somewhat "virtual" table is referred to as the *result set*.

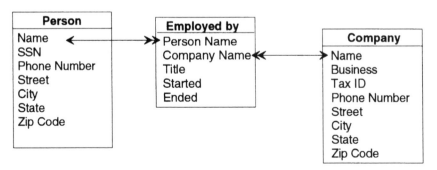

Figure 8.2   Functionally dependent entity.

Selection (Fig. 8.3) returns a result set that contains a subset of the table's rows based on the satisfaction of certain selection arguments. Projection (Fig. 8.4) limits the attributes of the result set to only a subset of the table's attributes. The join (Fig. 8.5) operation returns a result set where each row is made up of one or more different attributes from two or more tables where the rows in each table meet a specific argument criterion. The concatenate (Fig. 8.6) operation returns a result set containing the common attributes of all of the rows of two or more tables that meet the selection argument criteria.

SQL

SQL stands for structured query language and, according to the "rules" of the relational model, is the only language used to query and manipulate relational databases. SQL is made up of four basic types of commands:

- *DQL*—data query language. DQL statements are used to retrieve data from the tables that form the database. For example, the following illustrates a simple query that would retrieve a sorted list of "customer name" and "phone number" columns from all rows of the "customer" table where "customer status" was equal to "active":

```
Select Cust_Name, Ph_Nbr from Customer
Where Status = 'Active'
Order by Cust_Name
```

- *DDL*—data definition language. DDL statements are used to define the structure or schema of a database, define the types of columns to be stored in each table, create indexes, and define rules. For example, the following statements would create a customer table, define two columns for that table, and create a unique index on the "Cust_Name" column of the table.

```
Create Table Customer (Cust_Name Char(45), Ph_Nbr Char(20),
Status(1) );
Create Unique Index Cust_Name_Idx on Customer (Cust_Name);
```

- *DML*—data manipulation language. DML statements are used to maintain data stored in the database and include the

Person Table

Name	SSN	Phone	Employer
R. Nixon	010-23-4571	206-231-4523	ABC Corp
L. Johnson	123-34-8765	201-623-3421	Widgets R'Us
J. Kennedy	342-50-6754	412-091-6123	Widgets R'Us
J. Carter	500-51-3428	212-731-6500	ABC Corp
G. Bush	432-80-4521	210-345-4509	Brown & Assoc
B. Clinton	237-98-0987	206-309-2376	RAF, Inc.
R. Reagan	123-45-7896	900-432-4281	RAF, Inc..

Selection Operation

Select * From Person
Where Employer = ABC Corp

Result Set

Name	SSN	Phone	Employer
R. Nixon	010-23-4571	206-231-4523	ABC Corp
G. Bush	432-80-4521	210-345-4509	ABC Corp

Figure 8.3 Selection.

103

Person Table

Name	SSN	Phone	Employer
R. Nixon	010-23-4571	206-231-4523	ABC Corp
L. Johnson	123-34-8765	201-623-3421	Widgets R'Us
J. Kennedy	342-50-6754	412-091-6123	Widgets R'Us
J. Carter	500-51-3428	212-731-6500	ABC Corp
G. Bush	432-80-4521	210-345-4509	Brown & Assoc
B. Clinton	237-98-0987	206-309-2376	RAF, Inc.
R. Reagan	123-45-7896	900-432-4281	RAF, Inc...

Projection Operation

Select Name, SSN
From Person
Where Employer = ABC Corp

Result Set

Name	SSN
R. Nixon	010-23-4571
G. Bush	432-80-4521

Figure 8.4   Projection.

Person Table

Name	SSN	Phone	Employer
R. Nixon	010-23-4571	206-231-4523	ABC Corp
L. Johnson	123-34-8765	201-623-3421	Widgets R'Us
J. Kennedy	342-50-6754	412-091-6123	Widgets R'Us
J. Carter	500-51-3428	212-731-6500	ABC Corp
G. Bush	432-80-4521	210-345-4509	Brown & Assoc
B. Clinton	237-98-0987	206-309-2376	RAF, Inc.
R. Reagan	123-45-7896	900-432-4281	RAF, Inc...

Company Table

Name	Phone	Business
ABC Corp	106-531-4423	Retail
Brown & Assoc	206-309-2455	Legal
RAF, Inc.	314-532-4231	Manufacturing
Widgets R'Us	201-762-0081	Retail

Join Operation

Select Name, Employer, Business
From Person
Where Person.Employer = Company.Name

Result Set

Name	Employer	Business
R. Nixon	ABC Corp	Retail
L. Johnson	Widgets R'Us	Retail
J. Kennedy	Widgets R'Us	Retail
J. Carter	ABC Corp	Retail
G. Bush	Brown & Assoc	Legal
B. Clinton	RAF, Inc.	Manufacturing
R. Reagan	RAF, Inc...	Manufacturing

Figure 8.5   Join.

Person Table

Name	SSN	Phone	Employer
R. Nixon	010-23-4571	206-231-4523	ABC Corp
L. Johnson	123-34-8765	201-623-3421	Widgets R'Us
J. Kennedy	342-50-6754	412-091-6123	Widgets R'Us
J. Carter	500-51-3428	212-731-6500	ABC Corp
G. Bush	432-80-4521	210-345-4509	Brown & Assoc
B. Clinton	237-98-0987	206-309-2376	RAF, Inc.
R. Reagan	123-45-7896	900-432-4281	RAF, Inc...

Company Table

Name	Phone	Business
ABC Corp	106-531-4423	Retail
Brown & Assoc	206-309-2455	Legal
RAF, Inc.	314-532-4231	Manufacturing
Widgets R'Us	201-762-0081	Retail

Union Operation

Select Name, Phone From Persion
Union
Select Name, Phone From Company

Result Set

Name	Phone
R. Nixon	206-231-4523
L. Johnson	201-623-3421
J. Kennedy	412-091-6123
J. Carter	212-731-6500
G. Bush	210-345-4509
B. Clinton	206-309-2376
R. Reagan	900-432-4281
ABC Corp	106-531-4423
Brown & Assoc	206-309-2455
RAF, Inc.	314-532-4231
Widgets R'Us	201-762-0081

Figure 8.6 Concatenate.

ability to insert, update, and delete rows. For example, the following would change the status of all customers whose current status equals "temp" to "active":

```
Update Customer

Set Status = 'Active'
Where Status = 'Temp'
```

- *DCL*—data control language. DCL statements are used to grant specific levels of access to the data and define permissions that determine what data can be retrieved, updated, inserted, and deleted by individual users accessing that database. For example, the following would allow two people (PersonA and PersonB) to be able to select any row and any column, insert rows, and modify rows in the "customer" table but not allow them to delete rows:

```
Grant Select, Insert, Update
on Customer
to User1, User2.
```

SQL extensions. Standard SQL is not a procedural language and contains no flow of control (If...then...else, Do While, For Next, etc.) or device I/O statements, and although a number of math, string, and other functions are included in the standard it cannot, by any stretch of the imagination, be considered a full-featured programming language. To address this shortcoming, many relational database products extend the standard SQL with procedural constructs and provide a manner of attaching the resulting SQL procedures with the database itself.

Stored procedures. A stored procedure is essentially a program, usually stored in the database catalog, that combines standard SQL and vendor-specific extensions to perform application-specific processing on the database, executing directly on the server. Stored procedures can be initiated synchronously or asynchronously by clients directly through the database interface or triggered indirectly by significant database server events.

Triggers. A trigger is a special type of stored procedure that is initiated automatically by the database engine whenever a specific data modification event (such as an insert, modify, or delete) occurs. Triggers are often useful in domain and referential integrity enforcement and can also be used to initiate special additional processing that is transparent to the client application.

Discussion.   One of the major decisions that an application developer must make is how fully to exploit such vendor-specific extensions. On one hand, the database is often selected on the basis of the power and flexibility of its SQL implementation and to not take advantage of those extensions could be considered a waste of the product's functionality. On the other hand, the more an application uses vendor-specific extensions, the less transparent the database is to the application, restricting its portability to other database engines.

Database catalog

One of the major innovations of the relational model was the requirement that the "metadata," or definition of the database itself, also be stored in tables encapsulated within the database itself. Prior to the relational model the traditional hierarchical, network, and inverted-list database models required that the database be predefined, often through the execution of a compilation and linkage process. This approach of keeping the database definition separate from the actual database resulted in relatively static database structures that were difficult to change. The relational model, incorporating its own definition within itself, is far more dynamic, and changes to the catalog, where this definition is maintained, are immediately reflected in the database structure. The catalog of a relational database contains the definitions of all objects dealt with by that database, from table, column, and index definitions through users, user permissions, and data validation rules.

Indexing

The theoretical foundation of the relational model specifically excludes any consideration of the physical storage of the data or what physical mechanisms are utilized to retrieve that data from the media on which it is physically stored. Because of this relative freedom, the mechanisms used to physically retrieve and store data are one of the greatest differentiators between relational database products with the various vendors competing to optimize storage and retrieval through a number of different approaches. Indexing is one of the primary mechanisms by which this is accomplished. An index is essentially a mechanism to speed access to data by storing a "key" value paired with a "pointer" that points to the actual location of the data on the media where it is stored that is associated with that key value. Over the years a number of different approaches, B-trees, inverted lists, dense indexing, hashed indexes, and clustered indexes, to name just a few, have been developed to optimize the physical storage and retrieval of data. Each of these approaches have various strengths and weaknesses in specific situations. For example, hashed indexes are very fast at randomizing retrieving a single unique occurrence of a record but inefficient for sequential retrieval, by key value, of a range of records, which is a strength of the clustered-index approach. Most relational databases offer a range of different indexing options so that the developer can select an index type that will optimize the performance of data retrieval.

Concurrency

Concurrency is the mechanism by which the database controls multiple simultaneous accesses to the data so that all concurrent users of the database can be provided with a consistent view of the data at a specific point in time. It controls the process of updating, ensuring that no two users are updating the same data at the same time, and can, in more sophisticated implementations, allow the developer to control what "consistent" means in terms of synchronicity between data being updated and data being viewed. For example, if a particular row is in the process of being updated by one user, should another user be allowed to read that row at its current state or be forced to wait until the update to the row is applied? The goal is to provide as great a level of concurrency as possible while ensuring that a consistent view is maintained. Two different approaches are taken to provide high levels of secure concurrency.

Locking.   Locking is the process whereby the database reserves a specific data resource for the use of a single process until that process runs to completion or commits its work. At its simplest level, if process 1 selects row 25 for update, no other process would be allowed to select row 25 until process 1 committed its update. Locking strategies and options can become very sophisticated, depending on the database, and can be applied at different levels. For example, row locking provides the highest granularity of resource concurrency but often has a performance impact. Page-level locking reserves an entire page of physical storage, containing multiple records, when any one row stored within that page is updated. Page locking is generally faster because of the reduced overhead involved but can lead to greater occurrence of blocking because more "rows" are being locked at one time. The highest level of locking is at the table level, where all rows of the table are made unavailable until processing is committed.

Versioning.   Versioning is a completely different approach to providing concurrency. In versioning, the database makes "copies" of a row available to applications. Depending on the sophistication of the versioning mechanism, this approach may even allow concurrent updates to take place, which the database then sequentially applies to the underlying data. Versioning provides the greatest degree of concurrency but at a relatively high cost in resource consumption. Another disadvantage of versioning is that it introduces some interesting and complex issues regarding the interaction between a row's "state" and the consistency of its appearance to multiple concurrent viewers of that row.

Optimization

Query optimization is the mechanism by which the database attempts to define the fastest and most economical method of accessing the data necessary to respond to a query. In traditional databases actual pointers to related data's physical location were often embedded in the record itself. In this type of structure it is not necessary for the database to be able to "guess" at the fastest retrieval strategy that it already knew. In relational structures there are no physical pointers, other than those in the various indexes that may be used, in the rows that point to related rows. Consequently, a relational database needs to determine how to navigate the physical data space where its data is stored in order to return the requested result set.

Two basic approaches are taken to optimization. The first, rule-based or syntactical optimization, is the simplest and essentially defines its search strategy based on the structure of the query being requested. The second, and generally considered superior, approach is cost-based optimization. A cost-based optimizer seeks to find the least expensive strategy, in terms of physical I/O, to retrieving data based on what the database knows about itself. For example, a database using cost-based optimization knows that there are indexes available, it knows the approximate cardinality (i.e., how many of a given value are present) of each index, it knows about its utilization of the dataspace allocated to the database, and given these and other inputs can, theoretically, determine the fastest possible way of retrieving data.

Data types

This is a characteristic of relational databases that is becoming more and more important. Traditionally, the types of data stored in databases was pretty much limited to character strings, dates, and numbers with a variety of different data types available for storage and representation of these attributes in an efficient and appropriate manner. Over the last several years there has been a significant trend toward a need to store and manage such nontraditional data as large amounts of text, pictures, graphics, and digitally represented analog information (sound, video, etc.). As these needs have been recognized, relational database vendors have expanded the data types handled by their databases and have added functionality to manipulate these nontraditional data types.

Integrity constraints

There are two primary integrity constraints that should be implemented by any database management system, relational or not. The first is domain integrity. Domain integrity is the mechanism by which the database seeks to ensure that a given value to be inserted into a column is valid according to the rules, if any, that govern the valid values (the column's domain) for that column. Examples might include requirements that "status" be either "active" or "inactive," or that "salary" be greater than $1000 and less than $10,000.

"Referential integrity" deals with ensuring the completeness and validity of the relationships that have been defined through foreign keys. For example, Fig. 8.4 illustrates a relationship called "employer" between a person and a company. What rules should govern how a specific instance of this relationship is created? Must the company and person both exist before the relationship can be created? What happens to the relationship if the person instance is deleted? If the customer instance is deleted? The ANSI SQL Committee has recently defined a standard for how these integrity constraints should be implemented as extensions to the database catalog's metadata. Not all vendors have yet implemented those standards, so a relational database product that does not implement them will need to have the application itself, either in client code or in database coding mechanisms (triggers, stored procedures, etc.), take care of these integrity constraints.

Space utilization and optimization

The manner in which the database engine manages the actual storage space allocated to it is often a prime determining factor in its performance. The logical and theoretical foundations of the relational database standards do not specify physical storage constraints or specific approaches to physical implementation, and this is an area in which there is wide variability between commercial products. Some alternatives take the "black box" approach where the database engine controls all aspects of space allocation and usage, while others provide the database administrator with the ability to control many aspects of the allocation and therefore greater control over the database performance and optimization.

Object-Oriented Models

There exists a class of problems where the information needs cannot be adequately supported, because of their complexity, by the relational model. These problem spaces process extremely complex data structures and often display usage characteristics significantly different than those of traditional business systems. Computer-aided design and manufacturing, document publishing, expert systems, geographic information systems, and electronic performance support systems are all examples of applications that deal with complex data structures that do not easily map to simple tables and attributes. Object-oriented databases are distinguished from those based on the relational model by their incorporation of mechanisms to support encapsulation, inheritance, and complex attributes, which are actually collections of attributes or other objects.

Object-oriented database products, evolving out of object-oriented programming language research, are beginning to appear to address these more complex problems. Unfortunately, unlike the relational model, no widely accepted theoretical foundation for an object orientation yet exists and no standards have yet been defined for a common and consistent query language to manipulate the types of complex data structures typically found in object-oriented data models.

Further, the very features of an object-oriented database management system that provide its power and flexibility (classing, inheritance, encapsulation, collections, etc.) present some very formidable obstacles to implementing domain and referential integrity facilities that are essential to full database functionality. Although useful in specific circumstances it is unlikely, given the current situation, that object-oriented database management systems (OODMSs) will evolve beyond niche solutions to a very narrow range of problems. In many ways OODMSs are more of a step backward into the past of proprietary "closed" database systems accessible in only a few limited ways with no industry-wide standards to guide their usage or development. It is far more likely that current relational products will gradually provide more and more object-oriented extensions such as the binary large-object support (BLOS), stored procedures, triggers, and other enhancements within a framework that is based on evolving standards to meet a broad range of business problems.

Summary

Considerable experience has been gained by the vendors of relational database technologies over the last 15 years, and these products have matured significantly to the point today where the top tier of relational database software alternatives all offer functionally rich, high-performance, and stable database engines that are suitable choices for mission critical line-of-business client/server applications.

Building
Client/Server
Applications

9

Planning

So you want to develop client/server applications. Why? What organizational objectives will be met by the implementation of client/server technologies? Are these objectives critical to your organization? What technologies are currently in use to develop and deploy application systems? How are client/server technologies going to be integrated into your current environment? Do you care? What forms are your prospective client/server applications going to take? These are just a few of the questions you should answer before taking the plunge into client/server application development.

Planning Considerations

The time you spend finding the answers to these questions will be directly related to the use to which you will be putting client/server technologies. If your organization simply wants to experiment with the client/server approach, then not a great deal of time needs to be spent planning as the intent is merely to gain knowledge and expertise for use down the road. In this situation your time is better spent doing, not planning. On the other hand, if your organization is serious about utilizing client/server principles and technologies to either downsize current systems or integrate enhanced client/server functionality into current systems, then a certain amount of planning is definitely in order. Planning the initiation of client/server development efforts in any organization must address a number of critical issues, whether the development effort is strategic and impacts all aspects of the enterprise, tactical with a limited scope and time range, or merely an operational reaction to fulfill an immediate business needs.

Define the organizational objectives

It is essential for the developer to clearly understand the objectives the organization hopes to achieve with the deployment of client/server applications. Is the organization's objective to reduce overall information processing costs by migrating to more open, flexible, and less expensive client/server environments? If so, a fairly extensive enterprise-wide planning effort should be initiated to clearly define the long-term objectives and technological directions before initiating any significant client/server development efforts. On the other extreme, if the objective is simply to establish a more cost-effective, flexible, and easily used foundation for providing departmental system solutions of limited scope, then extensive enterprise-wide planning is probably contraindicated.

What type of solutions are to be delivered?

Despite the hype about downsizing and the death of the mainframe, not all client/server efforts are directed toward replacing existing, typically transaction-driven, business applications. Client/server applications come in as many different flavors as there are problems to solve. Client/server applications can often be more profitably deployed to extend the functionality of existing systems or to provide more cost-effective solutions for smaller, although no less important to their users, business needs that are not truly enterprise-wide in scope or mission-critical in importance. The nature of the problem space to be addressed will serve to shape the type of client/server solution, the tools selected, and the approach used by the project. In those environments where client/server technologies are just beginning to be introduced, the applications will tend to fall into one of four categories.

Decision support systems (DSS). These are applications in which their primary purpose is to provide the organization's decision makers with easily used access to information "about" the business in order to support analysis and monitoring of what has happened in the past, where "past" could mean anything from yesterday to last year. Also often referred to as *information warehouse applications,* the primary function of this category is to move information out of one or more environments, typically a production transaction processing environment where data is difficult to access, and into an environment where it is more readily available to those who need to analyze that data. The nature of the problem addressed by this type of application is primarily one of data modeling and database design, selection of appropriate end-user tools, and the transfer of information across technology boundaries. Specific applications in this category generally service small constituencies and are rarely enterprise-wide in scope.

Departmental support systems. These are applications in which their primary purpose is to automate one or more of the operational processes of a small group of users that, for reasons of scale, priorities, or other factors, have not been historically supported by production systems. This category of application typically incorporates some form of transaction processing and operational reporting and is often limited in scope to a specific operational process. Client/server applications in this category are often replacements for undocumented and no longer supported applications developed by the end users themselves. The nature of this problem is very similar to traditional development efforts, incorporating problem analysis, requirements definition, system and database design, construction and testing, and implementation. The primary differences are size, scope, and speed, with the development "team" usually consisting of only one person. Specific applications in this category generally service small constituencies and are rarely enterprise-wide in scope.

Transaction processing (OLTP). These are the typical "core" applications that serve to support the day-to-day operations of the business. Order entry, account management, sales and marketing, manufacturing resource planning, and financial applications are typical examples of "core" transaction processing systems that have traditionally been based on proprietary multiuser systems. Often referred to as *on-line transaction processing* (OLTP) systems, these applications are typically not limited to on-line transaction processing but also incorporate background or overnight processing, report generation, data transfer to and from other systems, and all the other functionality typically needed in support of day-to-day operations of an organization.

Electronic performance support systems (EPSS). This is a relatively new class of applications that is just beginning to come into use in larger organizations. EPSS applications combine elements of DSS, OLTP, computer-based training (CBT), and often real-time systems in order to provide the user with a single-system view of all the information—whether database, training manuals, operating procedures, problem identification, process management, or real-time monitoring—that the user requires to perform their function. Characterized by the ease of use and powerful information presentation capabilities they must provide, EPSS applications require the functionality and flexibility provided by client/server architectures.

Scope of impact

Determine the degree of impact the client/server implementation is likely to have in your organization. How much of your organization is likely to be impacted? Will the introduction of the technology touch every single facet of your operations, from mailroom clerk to chairman of the board? Will it be limited, at least initially, to isolated departments? Is it meant to be used by a specific class of users who may be limited in number but are spread throughout the organization?

Suitability of technological foundation

Assess your organization's current technological foundation. Is there currently a local area network in place? Is it adequate for supporting the type of client/server applications you intend to deploy within the next 6 months? Within the next 12 months?

Within the next 24 months? Assess the openness of that foundation and determine what standards are in place to assure interoperability, flexibility, and functionality.

Integration with current systems

Determine the degree of integration that will be needed between current systems and the client/server applications being contemplated. Will they coexist separately and independently? Will there be data flowing between the two? Will that data flow be unidirectional or bidirectional? Will the frequency be real-time, overnight, or quarterly?

Skill sets

Assess your organization's current inventory of skills and expertise at all levels. Are the users familiar with everyday use of workstations, graphical-user interfaces, and common productivity products? Are your developers tied to a single proprietary technology, or are they multiskilled in multiplatform technologies and tool sets? Do you have local area networking and systems integration skills require to operate in a heterogeneous multivendor environment?

The Planning Framework

Effective integration of new information technologies into the organization poses a challenge to any MIS department. Tasked with supporting current business operations and reducing project backlogs, it is difficult for MIS to focus resources on the technological, operational, and organizational issues that must be addressed to attain the benefits promised by client/server technologies. To achieve these benefits in a manner that is appropriate to their environment requires a level of planning in accordance with the considerations described above. This systems planning effort will generally take place somewhere within a three-tiered framework and, if it is to be effective, must be closely coupled with the organization's plans at the equivalent levels. This framework is made up of strategic, tactical, and operational levels.

Strategic planning

The purpose of strategic planning is to set goals and objectives. Strategic planning, at its simplest level, is simply to determine where you "want to be" within a reasonable length of time. In today's fast-changing and fiercely competitive business environment, this planning horizon is often limited to 3 to 5 years. On the organization side, planning at the strategic levels seeks to determine the organization's objectives in regard to products and services, operating policies, growth targets, market definition, and organizational reorganization. On the systems side, strategic planning consists of determining what information is needed by the organization to achieve those objectives, how that information needs to be structured, and how that information is to be delivered to where it is needed.

Tactical planning

The purpose of tactical planning is to determine how you are going to get from where you are to where you want to be, as defined by the strategic planning process. Tactical planning, often driven by budget issues, generally deals with time frames of 12 to 18 months. On the organization side, planning at the tactical level deals with the definition of requirements, financial forecasting, market forecasting, new-product introduction, project prioritization, and budget formulation. On the systems side, tactical planning deals with the evaluation and selection of technologies, the implementation of new technologies, identification and definition of new system development projects, and the training and development of personnel resources.

Operational planning

The purpose of operational planning is to implement tactical plans while simultaneously maintaining current activities. Operational planning is concerned with where you are today and generally deals with time frames from 1 week to 6 months. On the organization side, planning at the operational level deals with the allocation of resources, the support of daily activities, gathering information, producing products and services, and information monitoring and tracking. On the systems side, operational planning deals with maintaining current services at acceptable performance levels, allocation of resources to projects in progress, management of projects in progress, maintenance of currently installed technologies, installation and integration of new technologies, and the resolution and management of problems.

The introduction of client/server technologies can require, depending on organizational needs, directions, and expected usage—planning at every level of this framework. It is critically important to accurately and honestly determine the degree of planning necessary in your own specific organization. Because client/server technologies represent such a significant change, there will be a tendency in some organizations to automatically assume planning needs to begin at the strategic level. This assumption can lead to the formation of 6-month study groups, committees, and radical reassessments of direction in order to approve, or more likely disapprove, the deployment of the technology to service the limited needs of a small department. On the other hand, incorrectly assessing the impact of the technology and adequately planning for its integration can result in a proliferation of poorly designed, insupportable, and incompatible application environments isolated from each other by insurmountable technological boundaries.

Planning for Change

It is, quite literally, impossible to overestimate the impact on your organization of the change represented by client/server technologies. Further, this change extends far beyond the MIS department. It is not just the developers, operators, and management that needs to learn new technologies and ways of doing things but also the business users themselves. Internal MIS customers will be required to take increasingly active participation involvement in their systems, learn new tools, perform new activities, and accept greater responsibility for meeting their information and processing needs. Recognizing the importance of this factor and planning for change must be a critically important piece of all strategic, tactical, and operational plans. A number of conditions must exist for successful change to be implemented:

Pain. This is expressed as dissatisfaction with the current state. All levels of the organization, from those who do the work to those who direct and have the power to implement change, must be dissatisfied with how things are done.

Vision. There must be alternatives available to address the inadequacies and a clearly articulated vision of how those alternatives will improve the current environment.

Excitement. To implement change successfully requires not just the passive acceptance of change but the willing and enthusiastic participation in the process of change by all of the people impacted.

Trust. There must exist a level of trust between those who are directing the change and those who are the most impacted so that whatever is necessary to support the transition through the time of change will be provided.

It is a widely accepted truism that people resist change and that the greater the change, the more people will resist it. The primary impediment to change is fear. But it is not just "fear of change" itself but "fear of failure" that impedes change. People are fearful that they won't, at an individual level, be able to learn the new ways and will fail to make the transition. This is especially true in the current economic environment where companies are laying off thousands of workers and whole industries are disappearing from the American economy. Recognition of this basic reason for people's resistance to change is an integral part of planning for change. Planning for, and implementing, successful change requires that this basic fear must be addressed and the prerequisites for change be present and reinforced. A successful transition plan must address the following:

Training. A critically important factor in successful change is training. Training, done correctly, addresses the most common cause of "fear of failure" by providing people with the skills and knowledge required to make the leap to a new way of doing things. Because all people are different, it is essential to structure a training plan that addresses the many various ways in which different people acquire and assimilate new concepts and skills. An effective training plan incorporates many different approaches that interact to reinforce the acquisition of skills and knowledge. Formal classroom instruction is often effective for imparting general and basic skills to large groups of people in a highly structured environment. Unfortunately, that is where most training programs stop and also why most training programs are ineffective at preparing people for change. An effective plan must also incorporate self-paced instruction, on-the-job mentoring and support, and highly interactive peer-level review and feedback to support and reinforce what is learned in the classroom. Remember that the goal of the plan is to ensure that no one is left behind in the transition.

Experimentation.   It is essential that the transition plan not just allow for experimentation but encourage it. An essential part of the American archetype is that we almost never get it right the first time, and planners who ignore this basic cultural characteristic do so at their own peril. The plan must not only require experimentation but also provide channels for feedback so that the results of experimentation are as widely disseminated as possible and that those results are incorporated and assimilated into the plan itself.

Celebration.   A successful plan will also provide for regular and explicit celebration of both failures and successes. In many cases the failures that will be encountered as a normal and expected part of change transition are ultimately more important than successes. After all, it is from our failures that we learn the most. Celebration of failures also has the benefit of alleviating much of the "fear of failure" that serves to fuel people's resistance to change.

10

The Organizational Challenge

The main obstacles that large organization with traditional MIS departments and corporate data centers face when attempting to implement client/server technologies are not technological but political. True, the technologies involved are less mature and reliable. It is also true that the vendor support, although rapidly improving, is of significantly lower quality than that traditionally available from proprietary OEM technologies. But corporate data centers have successfully dealt with immature, unstable, and poorly supported technologies in the past. Most of the technologies taken for granted in the mainframe world today, such as fourth-generation languages (4GLs), database management systems (DBMSs), on-line transaction processing (OLTP), multichannel T1, and X.25, were immature and unstable not that long ago. So why is client/server technology proving so difficult to successfully integrate into the corporate-data-center world? Because client/server architecture represents a genuine paradigm shift in information processing. It is not simply a new and better way of doing an old job but a completely different job. Failure to recognize this fact and organize accordingly will doom many pilot client/server projects to painful failure. Three political problems must be addressed within the typical large organization's data center before client/server technology can be successfully integrated into corporate information systems.

The Corporate Data Center

Organization

The traditional corporate data center is organized to manage a world of proprietary hardware and software with well-defined and tightly controlled interfaces and coordinated software release levels. As illustrated in Fig. 10.1, this has resulted in an organization that is highly compartmented, with groups of deeply but narrowly skilled specialists operating within clearly understood boundaries defined by hardware and software components. Within even the best-managed data centers cross-functional teamwork is rare and intergroup communication generally limited to formal change-control committees and procedures. Because of the superficial similarity of client/server and mainframe architectures, traditional data center manage-

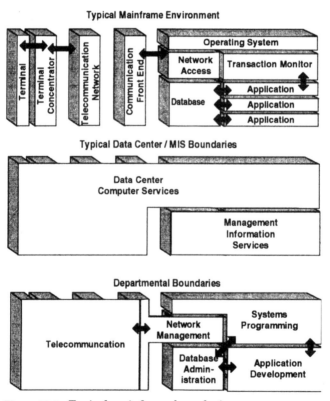

Figure 10.1   Typical mainframe boundaries.

ment often believes that client/server architectures can be implemented and supported using their current organizational model.

Unfortunately, the highly compartmentalized structure that works well in a homogeneous environment of well-integrated single-vendor proprietary hardware and software components is inappropriate for poorly integrated multivendor environments. Application of the mainframe-centric organizational model to client/server environment, as illustrated in Fig. 10.2, inevitably leads to serious disputes over the control and relative importance of the various components that go into making up a client/server implementation.

Who fixes the problem when the transport protocol for the network specified by the telecommunication group won't support the interprocess communication protocol required by the database management software specified by the development group? Who controls the installation of the specialized GUI dynamic link library needed to connect a development tool with the network operating system specified by the network man-

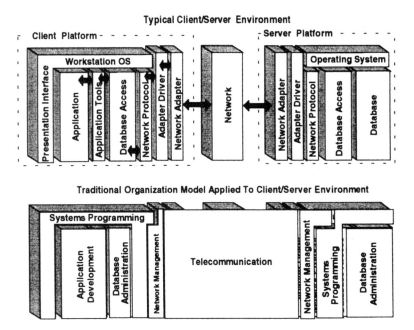

Figure 10.2   Classic organization in client/server environment.

agement group? When these issues arise, as they inevitably do in the initial client/server installation, win/lose issues of control and ego rapidly become more important than solving the technical problem. The managers ultimately responsible for resolving such issues may often believe it is not in their best interest to see client/server technology succeed. After all, the term *downsizing* applies to more than just hardware.

Resources

Given the organizational model, it appears logical to assign the telecommunication-communication, network, and systems gurus, with their networking, VTAM/NCP, and IBM systems software skills, to the installation and support of the new environment. Learning the new technology from the ground up, part-time because these are valuable people with real work to do in the production environment, these specialists are quickly confronted with the hardware and software simplicity, relative instability, nonexistent vendor support, and lack of problem resolution tools. They quickly conclude that the new technology just isn't ready for production yet. Further, these specialists must now share responsibility with developers, their traditional antagonists, in an environment characterized by fuzzy boundaries between components that are highly interdependent. The friction generated by this situation is worsened by the fact that the client/server developers, because they must interact in a far more intimate manner with the operating and network systems software, are often more knowledgeable in the new environment than their mainframe counterparts. With all of these personnel reporting to different managers, all with their own concerns and private agendas, the failure of the pilot client/server project is almost assured.

Functionality

The advent of client/server technology forces the data center organization to move into new functional areas within the corporation. Much of the promise of client/server lies in its ability to more tightly integrate mainstream mission-critical business applications with such desktop-based administrative, management, and planning tools as word processing, ad hoc numeric analysis, and graphics. These are functional areas traditionally shunned by corporate data centers. After all, if that functionality was really important, it would be on the mainframe, wouldn't it? This traditional attitude is what allowed end-user departments to take over the desktop, often to the extent of establishing and managing their own local area networks. These departments will often view client/server technology more as an extension of their own environment, not the data center's. With justification such departments will demand much greater participation in and control over client/server implementation. Having resisted end-user computing, or even any contact with end users, for years the traditional data center will often not be prepared to convince these departments that the data center can add any significant value to the process.

Discussion

How can traditional mainframe data center management looking to successfully implement client/server technologies address these issues? As in most such situations, there probably is no single right way to approach these problems. Different approaches will work (or not) depending on how well they match the reality of the organization and its commitment to evaluating the technology. But a number of steps, outlined below and explained in greater detail on the following pages, will serve to increase the likelihood of success:

- Define appropriate roles and develop an organization that is in closer alignment with the technological and functional boundaries of technologies being used.
- Honestly assess the skills available and put in place a plan to train personnel in the acquisition of new skills needed.
- Establish a clearly defined set of standards that are in accordance with the organization's technological direction.
- Establish a self-directed work-team approach to developing applications in close alignment with business needs using client/server technologies.

The keys to the successful introduction of client/server technology into an existing mainframe-centric environment are organizational flexibility and people, not technology. Those organizations that will succeed are those who are willing to make the fundamental changes necessary to adequately install, maintain, and support this environment.

Redefining the MIS Organization

In order to organize effectively to establish a maintainable technology foundation, develop and deploy appropriate applications, and support the operations of those applications in a client/server environment, it is necessary to define the organizational roles necessary to the new environment and clearly delineate the boundaries of responsibility. Although organizational forms will vary from situation to situation, those organizations with which I am familiar that have successfully introduced client/server technologies have generally implemented a structure defined along the boundaries illustrated in Fig. 10.3. This form structures responsibilities along boundaries that are reasonable and provide the personnel responsible with the span of control necessary to perform the activities associated with those roles.

Systems administration

The systems administration function is concerned with the management of the server hardware and software resources necessary to provide shared services to the applications and clients operating on the network. This responsibility extends from the evaluation, selection, and maintenance of the hardware itself plus all software operating with the server environ-

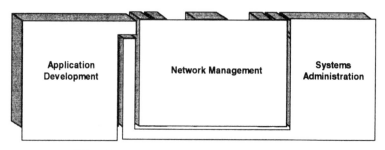

Figure 10.3   Client/server organizational model.

ment. This functional area is also responsible for the day-to-day operation of the server, controlling network and server access and security, allocation of server resources, performance and tuning, the network operating system, DASD management, capacity planning, and the installation and management of all server-specific application software including database management software, server communication gateways, e-mail services, and any other server software functions being performed. Roles typically found within this functional area include the following:

Hardware configuration and installation

Operating system (or network operating system) installation, maintenance, and tuning

Server application installation and configuration

Security administration and resource allocation

Network management

The network management function is concerned with the physical foundations of the network. The control extends from the network adapter card (server and client) through all transmission media, hubs, MAUs, repeaters, bridges, routers, and gateways that exist on the network connecting the clients and servers. This functional area is responsible for evaluation, selection, operation, troubleshooting, capacity planning, and performance optimization of all physical network components.

Equipment evaluation, selection, and installation

Network design

Network performance monitoring and tuning

Network capacity planning

Troubleshooting and problem resolution

Application development

The application development function is concerned with the development and integration of the applications and management of the client environment in which those applications operate. With the distinctions among traditional productivity applications (word processing, spreadsheets, etc.), development tools, and business applications becoming fuzzier by the day and the intimate relationship among workstation hardware, operating system, and application, it is essential that the application development function exercise control over the environment in which the major portion of that application operates.

Workstation and operating system configuration and installation

Application evaluation, selection, and installation

Systems analysis

Data modeling and database design

System design

User interface design

Programming

Skills Assessment and Training

It is impossible to overstate the importance of proper training in the successful implementation of client/server technologies. This training extends from the end user up through and including senior executives and is especially important for preparing current technical staff for the challenges represented by introducing client/server technologies into environments previously dominated by multiuser mainframe systems. Although technical personnel often pride themselves on being on the leading edge, it is often true that, as a group, they are among the most resistant to change in an organization. Experienced computer systems staff have spent years, sometimes decades, mastering complex mainframe, telecommunication, programming, and database technologies and are highly regarded within their organizations for their hard-won expertise. The introduction of radical change, as represented by client/server technologies, serves to invalidate much of that knowledge, and no one likes to start over.

There is no easy solution to this problem, but intensive training, focused on specific knowledge required to fulfill the responsibilities of assigned roles, is an absolute requirement to effect the transition of current technical staff into the client/server environment. The first step in this training should be an honest and complete assessment of the skills that are available within the organization and a determination of what is needed to fill the gaps. The next step is to fill the roles needed with new or existing staff and then initiate a training program focused on those role responsibilities that is designed to bring those staff up to the necessary level of expertise as quickly possible.

Establishing Standards

Assuming that you have the technological foundations in place that have been selected in accordance with the needs and technology directions of the organization (Chaps. 3 through 6), the last step in preparing for client/server development is the creation of those standards which will serve to provide a framework within which your developers can productively build and deliver client/server applications. At a minimum, there should be standards in place to govern:

Tool usage standards. Establish guidelines that define the tools to be used for the various application categories using client/server technologies. For example, the Excel/Q&E combination might be specified as appropriate for ad hoc query, numeric analysis, and generation of graphics based on server-supplied data. OLTP applications meeting mission-critical operational needs might instead specify the use of tools such as "C," Smalltalk [developed by A. Kay and others at Xerox's Palo Alto (Calif.) Research Center (PARC)], or Powersoft's Powerbuilder.

Source code management. Establish strict standards concerning the storage, check-in, and check-out of source code.

Interprocess communication. Establish standards to guide the standard uniform usage of the interprocess communication facilities available in the client and server environments. Examples include dynamic data exchange (DDE) and network DDE, object linking and embedding (OLE), named pipes, and remote-procedure calls (RPCs).

Naming standards. There should be in place a complete set of standards to guide the naming and identification of every object of any kind used within the development environment.

Objects that should be covered include, but are not necessarily limited to, programs, modules, windows/forms, form fields, program variables, functions, libraries, databases, tables, stored procedures, data elements, and files.

Documentation standards. For each category of client/server application, define the documentation that is required, at a minimum, to accompany that application. For a simple query and analysis application, that minimal documentation may be no more than a paragraph. The full OLTP mission-critical application might require detailed requirements regarding definition, structured technical documentation, operational turnover procedures, a user manual, and on-line user help facilities.

Change control and release management. One of the biggest operational problems to be faced by client/server developers is the synchronized and controlled release of their applications across all the clients on which they must be installed. The mainframe application developer lives within a highly structured environment where change is often rigidly controlled by other departments. The client/server developer, working in a far more flexible environment, must consciously take a disciplined approach to introducing change, and although there are automated tools available to distribute application changes, these do not take the place of the reasonable and sound change management procedures necessary to protect the stability of the environment.

Quality assurance. Client/server or mainframe, it doesn't really matter, because software quality must be planned into a development project from the beginning, engineered into the final application through the observance of quality goals, standards, and procedures. Client/server technologies do not obviate the need for strict quality assurance; indeed, in many ways more attention must be paid to client/server applications because of the complexity of the underlying foundation technologies.

User interface. Last, but hardly least, user interface (UI) standards and guidelines are critically important early in the client/server implementation process. These standards and guidelines are also among the hardest to define and agree on despite having many industry standard examples. Unfortunately, every developer and most end users believe themselves to be UI design experts, and few, if any, are. UI design is coming to be recognized as a specific discipline, grounded in theories of human cognition and psychology. Although most organizations cannot afford, or do not recognize, the need for this expertise, it is still important to define a standard that will govern the consistent look, feel, and interaction of applications with their users.

Redefining Systems Development

The basic defining problem with systems development, from the business user's perspective, is that systems development is out of touch with the needs of the business, and this perception is largely justified by the track record of most large systems development organizations over the last 10 years. The reasons for this are many and varied, and some are actually true. But the introduction of client/server technologies and workstation-based development environments are removing most of the technical justification for keeping the developers in the back room. This new found flexibility frees the traditional MIS organization to experiment with new approaches to delivering service to their primary constituencies. An approach that is uniquely well suited to the client/server approach is also one that is delivering a true revolution in the American workplace.

Work teams

An endemic problem faced by American industry and business is employee productivity. The topic of endless books, management treatises, articles, and studies, this problem also exists to an equal or greater extent in the area of systems development and for much the same reasons. One innovative way in which this problem is being addressed in the industrial sector is through the implementation of self-directed work teams, and this approach promises to be equally effective when applied to the development of client/server applications.

Self-directed work teams are more than just a different name for the traditional development project teams. As implemented in industry, a self-directed work team is a group of 5 to 15 people tasked with total responsibility for turning out a product or service, from concept through design and into production. The key words here are "total responsibility." The work team is responsible for planning the project, setting priorities, determining the objectives, assigning the tasks, and performing the work. Self-directed work teams are, by definition, made up of cross-trained multiskilled individuals who apportion the work internally and share in both the challenging and not-so-challenging activities associated with the project.

While a traditional systems development project involves many different organizations, each with differing aims and agendas, and is structured to depend on the skills of multiple supporting groups, the successful self-directed work team is structured to be essentially self-sufficient and as independent as possible. Even when the work team does, of necessity, need outside assistance from a supporting organization, the nature of that interaction is controlled by the work team, demanding a specific level of service and being free to go elsewhere for the support if not satisfied with the service provided. This is a far cry from the typical project team that is at the mercy of some other group's priorities, politics, or agenda when there is a need for some technical assistance beyond the project team's expertise.

Self-directed work teams are about independence and doing whatever is necessary to getting the job done. As such teams co-opt many of the functions and responsibilities of line and middle management and cross organizational boundaries, they are often perceived as threatening to those same management levels. But if an organization can overcome the obstacles to such teams, the benefits can be enormous. There is widespread documentation of these benefits in the industrial sector as many major *Fortune* 100 companies have reported productivity gains of 25 to 50 percent over periods as short as 18 months. Much of these gains come simply from the reduction in bureaucracy, with decision-making cycles reduced from months to days. Further, such teams tend to encourage the experimentation that leads to rapid failure, which leads to greater understanding, which ultimately leads to quicker success and higher-quality end results.

Establishing such teams is not an easy matter, especially in the traditional MIS environment where management tends to be autocratic and top-down and where the relationship between MIS and the business are characterized by "us vs. them" mindsets. From the business's perspective MIS personnel are those people who talk in jargon, don't understand the business, make little effort to truly understand the user's needs, and have consistently failed to deliver what they promised. From the MIS perspective, business users are those people who are demanding, unable to explain what they want, ignorant of the technical issues and limitations of what they ask for, and just generally unappreciative of the major efforts put forward in their behalf. To set up such teams in this environment requires a very real commitment from MIS management, business management, and the team members themselves. The general roles to be played by members of such a team include:

- *Area experts*—the representatives of the user constituency for which the team is to produce a product and who are responsible for clearly and concisely defining the problems to be addressed and solutions to be delivered. They must be knowledgeable in the business, fully conversant with the problems to be addressed, and committed to delivering a solution that will address those problems.

- *Data analyst*—the person(s) with skills in information modeling, data analysis, and database design who has (have) deep expertise in the analytical and technical skills required to determine information requirements and reformulate those requirements into physical database designs that will serve to meet those requirements.

- *User interface designer*—a person with skills in determining user needs, presenting the solutions to those needs in terms of a human/machine interface that is consistent, friendly, and usable by the designated constituency and technically feasible to develop.

- *Architect*—the person with deep technical design skills who is responsible for all aspects of the technical design of the resulting systems solution, defining the necessary systems interfaces, liaison with technical resources outside of the group to coordinate technical activities, and is further responsible for removing any technical obstacles to the achievement of the team's objectives.

■ *Developer*—the application programmer(s) tasked with the responsibility of building and testing the application in accordance with the directives and specifications of the user interface, system, and database design.

Depending on the size and nature of the project, two or more of the roles can be played by a single person, or there can be several individuals playing each role. One of the main keys to team performance, though, appears to be size. The most effective teams rarely exceed 20 people and more commonly consist of 10 or fewer people. The selection of team members, especially for the first such teams to be used, must be done carefully. A number of characteristics are important:

■ Skill and experience in a designated role

■ Ability to embrace change and dissatisfaction with the status quo

■ Eagerness to learn new skills and interact intensively with people from different backgrounds

■ Ability to compromise and open to new ideas

■ Enough confidence to put forward ideas and voice opinions

From the basic setup the work team appears very similar to a typical systems development project team. The differences lie in the execution. This is meant to be a self-contained, independent, and self-directed team. It is not a group of individuals from different departments who meet once a week or so and then go back to their departments. This is a team that works together, preferably in the user constituency's area, 8 hours a day, 5 days a week until the objective is achieved. It reports only to the executive sponsor of the team and is responsible only to that sponsor. While all team members are selected for the specific skills they bring to assigned roles, the actual responsibilities, as assigned by the team, will include activities that are outside those roles. Team members are responsible for learning such skills as necessary to pitch in and assist other team members and are further responsible for teaching their own skills to other members within the group. Teams leaders are not appointed but evolve out of the team's recognition of special skills, and leadership tends to rotate among team members as the work progresses through different phases that stress different skill sets. There is no project manager or equivalent. The team, as a whole, is responsible for its work, not one individual. The team either achieves its objectives as a group or fails to achieve its objectives as a group. After initial setup, training, and a breaking-in period, the team is responsible for its own makeup. Members not performing to the team's satisfaction can be removed from the team on the team's own authority. The team has final approval over all replacements or additions.

It is the executive sponsor's responsibility to set the goals of the team, clearly define the boundaries of its authority and responsibility, facilitate any extraorganizational cooperation necessary to support the team, and monitor the performance of the team against the objectives being set. The executive sponsor identifies "what" is to be accomplished; the team decides "how" it is to be accomplished. Team member performance is not evaluated by their nominal department heads but by the team sponsor and other team members from whom the sponsor will solicit formal input and feedback.

Work-team phases. When work teams are first introduced and as new teams are formed, there is a basic three-stage life cycle through which new teams normally progress. Management and team sponsors must be aware of this life cycle and recognize that these stages are an essential and natural aspect of a team's growth, despite the pain and awkwardness often experienced by everyone involved.

Phase I: confusion. The initial period of a self-directed work team's life is characterized by confusion, anarchy, fear, and suspicion as the team members try to work out their basic interactions, develop plans, and, most importantly of all, develop trust in senior management that they have not been cast adrift and begin to realize that they really do have the authority to balance their responsibilities. The role of management and team sponsors at this stage is to provide the team with clearly defined objectives, boundaries to their authority, and training in personal and team interaction, and to remove the "fear of failure" implicit in such a radical change.

Phase II: coalescence. Phase II represents the team's adolescence as it begins to coalesce, generally around a natural leader or strong personality, and becomes comfortable in its empowerment to actually implement change and progress toward its objectives. The team begins to experiment with potential approaches and solutions to the problems assigned and almost invariably fails several times. This failure is a critical part of the growth process as it provides an opportunity for the team to come together to overcome adversity. Of almost equal importance is the team's recognition that those failures are not being "punished" by management but actually celebrated as good tries, thereby building trust between the team and management and removing the "fear of failure" that is the primary impediment to progress in today's workplace. The primary role of management at this point in the team's growth is to be supportive.

Two fairly common developments generally occur at this stage. The natural "leader" around which the team has coalesced may develop into the team's "manager," a seriously adverse condition for a self-directed team. Careful attention must be paid to how leadership is being used within the team and whether it is impeding a free flow of ideas and alternative solutions. It may be necessary to counsel the leader or refresh the team's training as a whole to assure a balanced sharing of responsibility and authority. Self-directed teams are, by definition, not managed in the traditional autocratic sense, from either within or without.

The second trend to be on the look out for is a developing sense of "us vs. them" as the team comes together and begins to see itself as something apart from and independent of the organization from which it sprang. Again, this is a natural, healthy, and expected development. Management and team sponsor must take special care at this point to redirect the team's focus and ensure that its interaction internally within its sponsoring department and externally with other teams is open and cooperative instead of closed and competitive.

Phase III: maturity. As the team matures, its leadership tends to shift and rotate throughout the team as specific skills and knowledge become increasingly and decreasingly more important as objectives are achieved and activities change their focus. Team interaction with its constituency and other teams is open and cooperative, and the teams begin to initiate actions and projects within the boundaries of their assignment. At this phase the teams are almost wholly self-directed and management's role tends to be solely goal setting and facilitation.

The work-team function within the organizational model. Integrating a work-team approach into traditional system development organizations can be a very traumatic or relatively easy transition, depending on your current organization. Most system development organizations tend to follow one of two basic organizational models. The first is a basic functional alignment with the business with specialized supporting groups broken out along a different path. Illustrated in Fig. 10.4, this model breaks out into some form of information resource management or database administration group, a tools and technologies group of high skilled technicians, and a number of development groups that are organized along business lines (finance, human resources, manufacturing, etc.), each of which is responsible for both development and maintenance of systems supporting its business units. It is fairly simple, organizationally, to develop this form into groups of self-directed work teams attached to the business units themselves, supported by the two remaining groups who provide services to the work teams when their particular skills are called on.

The second form, illustrated in Fig. 10.5, is an outgrowth of the "assembly line" approach to systems development and attempts to organize the department around the kinds of work and requests that are generated from the business units. It is

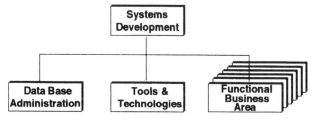

Figure 10.4 Business functional model.

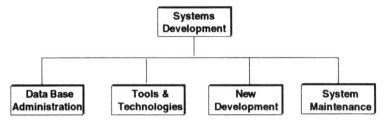

Figure 10.5   MIS functional model.

very difficult to install self-directed work teams within this type of organizational model. The first reason for this difficulty lies in the fact that the very nature of the organization has served to discourage close user/developer interaction and hindered developer identification with specific business units. Further, this organizational model tends to produce more "specialists" who are deeply but narrowly skilled and less generally qualified to add value to a work team throughout a system's life cycle.

Establishing a self-directed work-team approach is not an easy task and is fraught with risk, but, for those who are successful, the benefits are proportional and proved by a vast number of companies who have applied the principles throughout their organizations. I encourage anyone wishing to implement this approach to review the case studies of others who have taken this direction and the various industry and professional sources that address this approach.

Getting Started

Now you have everything in place. The technological foundations are installed, integrated, and operating according to specification. You have initiated or are in the process of planning the organizational changes that will be required, training has been completed, and standards and procedures have been defined. What are you going to pick for your first application to prove the concepts? There are a number of schools of thought on this issue. Many believe that a "toy" application should be developed first in order to gain practical experience with the least risk. Unfortunately, in this day of leaner MIS departments, chronic resource shortages, and 10-year project backlogs it is difficult to justify spending time on toy applications. Others say toy applications teach little, don't serve to fully test the concept, and believe a mission-critical OLTP application should be used as the pilot application. This theory has its own problems, not the least being risk and serious exposure to adverse political factors. My own experience indicates that one approach that has proved effective for introducing client/server technologies in many organizations is to select and schedule a series of increasingly difficult projects, categorized by type of application and scope of impact, that tend to successively build on prior success and knowledge gained while serving to limit the problem areas with which each project has to deal.

For example, consider addressing a decision support problem for the first several client/server efforts. There are always a number of backlogged requests in any sizable organization to provide the end user with direct access to what is commonly referred to as "production" data. Select one of these requests that will provide a significant benefit to an important user constituency of small size (e.g., 10 to 20 users). This type of application has several advantages.

1. It does not generally entail significant problem analysis, process management assessment, reengineering, requirements definition, or other activities that tend to extend the early phases of a systems development life cycle.

2. It is primarily a data analysis and database design problem, not a system design problem, with a short system development life cycle.

3. It deals with known data, in a known format, in a known location.

4. The major technical problem to be faced is extracting the data from its current location and transferring it across a technology boundary.

5. It introduces the user community to the power and flexibility of standard desktop applications when their reach is extended to production data.

6. The application developers gain knowledge of the performance characteristics of the database management software and server configuration and prove the reliability of the foundation technologies under light usage.

7. The existing multiuser system's technology and data are leveraged in a manner that enhances the value of both the client/server technology and the existing technology.

Once your developers are comfortable with the characteristics of the database management software, the use of desktop applications to access server data, and the reliability of the foundation technologies move on to a more full-function departmental application. Again, there are almost always some opportunities in the backlog, and with a little planning it is sometimes possible to leverage one of the earlier decision support efforts by extending its functionality with departmental transaction processing. Again, limit the size of the expected constituency to approximately 10 to 20 users. This project introduces more complexity; it will require analysis, requirements definition, system and database design, programming with an appropriate professional tool set, and, in general, the exercise of a full, although short, systems development life cycle. Besides providing the users with needed functionality, this second project achieves the following objectives for the developers:

1. Exercises the full set of systems development skills in a client/server environment but within a context and problem space consciously limited to a small user consistency.

2. Provides an opportunity to field-test new methodologies such as rapid prototyping that are uniquely suited to client/server development within a controlled and limited environment.

3. Introduces developers to the selected professional tool set (languages, design aids, debuggers, etc.).

4. Provides practice and experience in data modeling, physical database design, concurrency analysis, and database performance tuning in a client/server environment.

5. Enhances knowledge of the operating and performance characteristics of the database management software and server in concurrent transaction processing, ad hoc query, and reporting conditions.

After a progression of several successful decision support and departmental systems, you should have a team of developers comfortable with the tools and environment, familiar with the operating and performance characteristics of the server, and experienced in methodologies suited to client/server development. Not only have you gained experience in the technologies but applications of real value have been provided to the organization, and, assuming that the direction is to deploy mission critical client/server applications, the team can begin addressing larger problems with much of the risk factor removed. It can be surprising at how quickly this process can be competed with 5 to 10 small decision support and departmental applications delivered in 6 months to a year, approximately the same amount of time it would take a typical large multiperson mission-critical project to get through analysis, requirements, and design.

Chapter

11

Methodology

The use of client/server technologies does not do away with the need for adequate problem analysis, needs definition, and system design skills. The basic problem of system development, whether client/server or mainframe, still remains the definition of "what" needs to be delivered. The activities performed in the identification and definition of this "what" have traditionally been structured into a methodology. A methodology is simply a set of well-documented steps that are to be performed in order to achieve some objective. Systems development methodologies are attempts to refine and discipline the process of developing an information system into a standard set of procedural steps in order to enable the developer to more clearly understand the problem space being addressed and the solutions that are required. Over the years these efforts to apply discipline to the "art and craft" of information systems development have resulted in a host of different and competing methodologies, all promising to shorten development cycles and increase the quality of the resulting product. Unfortunately, few of these "canned" approaches delivered on their promises.

The reasons for this failure are many and not always obvious. At least they weren't to those of us trying to use them at the time. Almost uniformly, these methodologies took innovative techniques defined by such pioneers as Djikstra, Constantine, Gane and Sarson, and others and attempted to codify them in rigid linear step-by-step frameworks that were based on five fundamental assumptions:

- All requirements can be prespecified.
- Users are expert at specification of their needs.
- Users and developers are both good at visualization.
- The project team is capable of unambiguous communication.
- A single methodology and tool set is inherently valid for all systems development efforts.

As it turns out, none of these basic assumptions is even close to being true. Requirements change rapidly over time. End users rarely know "what" they want until they see it, and the mere process of seeing it will tend to change their perspective of what it is they really need. It is impossible to adequately capture, on paper or in other documentation, the complexity of how a system will work and be used by end users and ridiculously optimistic to expect end users to be able to visualize how a system will look and work on the basis of paper and drawings. Historical analysis indicates that not only are project teams incapable of unambiguous communication, they often find any form of meaningful communication, ambiguous or otherwise, to be a difficult achievement.

In addition to these false assumptions, a number of other, more subtle, causes for the failures of traditional methodologies are beginning to surface based on research into cultural archetypes performed by J. Adrian Desmond of the University of Chicago and Dr. G. C. Rapaille of Archetype Studies International. Archetype studies have been used for years by American companies attempting to make their products more "salable" in other cultures. Recently these studies and their conclusions are beginning to play a big role in quality improvement activities throughout American industry. This is not an appropriate place for a detailed discussion of these findings and I would heartily recommend *Incredibly American; Releasing the Heart of Quality* by Marilyn Zuckerman and Lewis J. Hatala, ASQC Press, 1993, and *Archetypes and Ancestors* by J. Adrian Desmond, University of Chicago Press, 1984, for those wishing more information in this area.

To synopsize an entire field of study, cultural archetypes are essentially shared fundamental and almost unconscious characteristics that drive basic actions, reactions, and perceptions of the members of a culture. Such characteristics appear to be acquired at an early age, are reinforced throughout adulthood, and they vary significantly from culture to culture. In a very real sense these archetypes form our basic natures as members of a given culture and appear to be remarkably consistent within a culture across socioeconomic, racial, religious, and other obvious segmentations. What American quality improvement research is showing is that different cultures approach the "quality problem" in different ways according to their archetypes or basic natures. So, what are the American archetypes that appear to define our basic natures? Those most directly impacting how we should approach systems development are:

- Americans don't expect things to work the first time.

- Americans like to experiment, constantly trying new approaches to problems until a solution is found.

- The archetypical American cultural hero is the person who tries and fails, keeps trying, and eventually overcomes adversity to achieve a goal. Failure in and of itself is not bad; giving up is.

- Perfection is something that is rarely worth the effort.

- Americans have a short attention span, tending to lose their focus and interest during any protracted effort.

Given these basic characteristics, is it surprising that traditional systems development methodologies failed to deliver the promised productivity and quality? These methodologies are all based on the premise that you need to do it right the first time. Our basic cultural characteristics tell us this is impossible. Further, the linear, step-by-tedious-step phased nature of these methodologies, as illustrated in Fig. 11.1, virtually guarantees protracted development periods during which project teams, users, and managers all basically just lose interest.

A methodology that will better fit the archetype, incorporate proven total quality management and continuous improvement techniques, and leverage the advantages of client/server technologies concepts will follow a significantly different pattern, as illustrated in Fig. 11.2. This illustrates the fact that most significant projects are really made up of three tightly coupled but

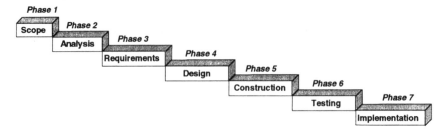

Figure 11.1   Traditional methodology phases.

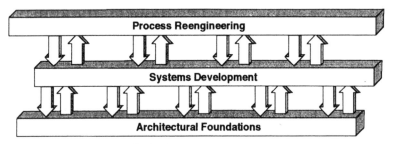

Figure 11.2   A more realistic view.

roughly concurrent legs dealing with different aspects of the solutions.

The process reengineering leg of the project is concerned with identifying and defining the problems to be addressed, gaining a broad understanding of the current situation and identifying the changes that must be made, defining and prototyping many different solutions until an optimal solution is determined, developing the optimal solution, implementing that solution into the operational processes, and then monitoring and making continuous improvements to the new processes.

The systems development leg of the project is concerned with modeling the information and workflows necessary to implement the solutions, prototyping the various solutions until an optimal solution is determined and the requirements of that solution are specified, designing and implementing a quality system to provide support as necessary and specified by the final prototype, implementing that systems solution in coordination with the new process solution implementation, and continuously enhancing and extending the functionality of the resulting system in coordination with the ongoing continuous improvement of the new process solutions.

The architectural leg of the project is concerned with identifying and validating the tools to be used in building the application, selecting and prototyping the client, network, and server technologies to be used in both prototyping and building the application, defining the manner in which the components of the application will be packaged and interact (i.e., physical system design), finalizing design, benchmarking, and implementing required data structures (i.e., physical database design), determining the distribution of data and function across the network, designing and implementing all external system interfaces, ensuring that enterprise standards are being adhered to, and preparing the final production-ready deliverable for turnover to operations. During continuous improvement the architectural leg of the project will monitor and tune database performance, optimize application resource usage where necessary, and monitor and call attention to any network capacity problems.

In addition to their tightly coupled concurrency, each of these legs is internally cyclic, going through four continuous stages, as illustrated in Fig. 11.3, and explained in greater detail below.

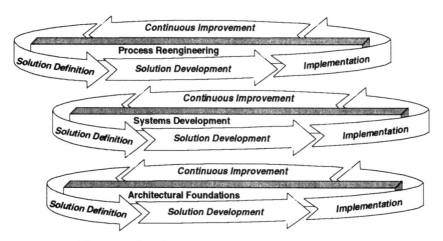

Figure 11.3   The natural cycle.

Solution Definition

Process reengineering

The solution definition stage of the process reengineering leg of the project deals with problem identification and solution determination, and is broken into three primary activities.

Identifying the problem(s). The first step in this stage is identification of the problem(s) that is (are) to be addressed. In any given problem space there are generally a multitude of problems to be addressed. The first step in the process is to identify those root causes that are key to providing the greatest benefit with the least expenditure of effort. This step begins by gathering as much data as possible concerning existing problems, potential opportunities for improvement, and builds a complete understanding of the current environment, workflows, and processes. The primary deliverable of this step is a concise definition of the problems, and opportunities for improvement.

Determining root causes. Each problem is examined in terms of the current environment and all possible causes of the problem are identified and verified. Causes are described and classified into one of eight categories: process, equipment, personnel, material, management, data, metrics, or physical environment. Relationships between the causes identified and the recognized effects of those causes are identified and quantified by strength of association. On the basis of this analysis, determine the root causes of the most significant problems. Prioritize the root causes in terms of their contribution to the significant problems. Identify those root causes that are within the boundaries of the work team's authority to address. The primary deliverable of this step is a concise identification, description, and prioritization of the relevant root causes.

Defining solution(s). The work team evaluates a wide range of alternative solutions to address the significant root causes. The most promising of the alternatives are prototyped for their suitability and ability to address the root causes. As each alternative prototype fails, lessons are learned about what worked and what didn't and other alternatives are modified to incorporate these lessons and prototyped again. This process continues until a solution or set of solutions are identified as those necessary to correct the root cause(s) of the problem(s). Surviving solutions are evaluated in terms of ease of implementation, negative side effects and by-products, consequences of implementation failure, ability of the work team to implement the solution, cost, and time to implement. The optimal solution is identified and a set of requirements for implementing that solution documented. The primary deliverable of this step is a complete description of the solution(s) to be implemented and an action plan for their full development and implementation within the workplace.

System development

The solution definition stage of the system development leg of the project is initiated with or very shortly after the beginning of process reengineering and proceeds in coordination with and support of those activities. It is broken into three basic activities.

Recovering current system design. The first step in this stage is basically a review of the current systems support being provided within the problem space and documentation of the current functions, technologies, and information structures being used by or potentially impacted by the processes under study. The primary deliverable of this step is initial population of a design repository with descriptions of information currently maintained and used.

Determining user needs. This step deals with gaining a thorough understanding of the problem space and the root causes being identified as potential opportunities for improvement. A model of the current processes and workflows and an initial information model of the main business objects identified as within the problem space is produced to verify understanding and assist the reengineering effort in quantifying root causes and identifying potential solutions. Initial prototypes of human/system interfaces are prepared in coordination with solution prototyping to determine feasibility, usability, and suitability of system support for the solutions being analyzed.

Defining functional requirements. This step deals with completion of the information model, development of a fully specified process or workflow model of the optimal solution, a completed prototype of the automated functions determined as necessary to support the optimal solution, a fully documented set of requirements describing the functionality to be provided by automated systems, and a detailed action plan indicating how the system to meet those requirements will be developed in coordination with the solution implementation plan.

Architecture

The solution definition stage of the architectural leg of the project is initiated with or very shortly after the beginning of process reengineering and proceeds in coordination with and support of those activities. It is broken into three basic activities.

Reviewing current technologies. The first step in this stage is basically a review of the technologies in use. Current workstation hardware and software are cataloged and evaluated for obsolescence and compliance with enterprise standards. Network connectivity and current system platform technologies are assessed and evaluated against enterprise plans and directions, and potential external interfaces are identified and researched.

Determining appropriate technologies. This step compares currently used technologies against enterprise directions and plans, evaluates the potential of both current and potential replacement technologies to meet the requirements of the optimal solutions being developed within the reengineering leg, prototypes viable solutions, and selects and installs appropriate technologies to meet the needs of those solutions.

Development tool selection. In coordination with the system development leg, potential development tools and technologies are evaluated against the projected needs of the optimal solutions being defined within the reengineering leg and appropriate development tools and technologies are selected and installed. Where necessary, system development personnel are trained in the effective use of the tools selected. Relevant enterprise standards are identified and reviewed.

Solution Development

Process reengineering

The solution development stage of the process reengineering leg of the project deals with developing pilots of the new workflows and processes required by the defined solutions, preparation of documentation and training programs for implementation of the solutions, and determination of the quality metrics that will be used to judge the effectiveness of the optimal solutions after their implementation. This stage consists of three primary activities.

Piloting the solutions. The first step in the piloting of the optimal solutions is to verify their adequacy and completeness. Adjustments are made as they are identified and, where necessary, are communicated to the systems development leg for inclusion into the system design.

Document evaluation metrics. Review the initial problem and root cause documentation and quantify the improvements that are to be expected through implementation of the optimal solutions. Develop and pilot the test methods to be used to gather postimplementation quality statistics.

Training preparation. Identify specific areas needing educational and training support to provide transition assistance to personnel impacted by the optimal solution changes. Develop appropriate classroom curriculum, prepare training materials, develop and qualify designated mentors, and finalize training action plan.

System development

The solution development stage of the system development leg is concerned with implementation of the physical database structure, construction and testing of the system in accordance with the architectural specifications provided by the architectural leg, development and testing of the conversion functions required to facilitate migration to the new system, and execution of the migration and conversion plan. It is broken into four basic activities.

Building physical database structure. The first step in this stage is implementation of the final physical database structure, coding and testing of all server-based application functions (stored procedures, triggers, user-defined functions, etc.).

Constructing the application. This activity involves the construction and unit testing of all modules of the application's architecture as designed within the architectural leg.

Testing the application. This activity involves the integration (i.e., module to module), system (i.e., function to function), and performance (i.e., benchmarking) testing of the application. Final usability, functionality, and acceptance testing is performed with the initial set of designated mentors in coordination with the reengineering leg.

Constructing and testing conversion functions. This activity, which often runs concurrently with the other development activities, task-codes and tests the conversion functions necessary to effect migration of data and functionality from the previous system (if any) to the new system.

Architecture

The solution development stage of the architectural leg is concerned with the physical design and specification of the application and database; the physical design, construction, and testing of all interfaces to external systems; the installation, integration, and testing of any new workstation, server, or networking technologies being used; and the development and documentation of a complete conversion plan. It is broken into six basic activities.

Completing the physical database design. Implement the final logical database design as specified. Prototype and benchmark the application's known highˇ-volume and heavy-use data access patterns. Generalize logical database design, and make adjustments in planned redundancy, indexes, and physical storage allocation's until the performance targets of the application are achieved. Complete physical database design and specify all database resident control and API mechanisms (stored procedures, triggers, etc.). Determine and map physical data distribution over the network and, if necessary, specify synchronization mechanisms.

Completing the application architecture. Package application functions into modules and subtasks, define intermodule message format standards and valid process flows, determine distribution of application functions across the network, and identify, define, and specify reusable resources. Verify adherence to appropriate enterprise standards and procedures.

Developing the conversion plan. Identify and define existing data sources that will migrate to the new application. Map existing data sources to their equivalents in the new database and specify all conversion, synchronization, and timing considerations. Determine the nature of the conversion (i.e., parallel vs. immediate cutover) and document a fall-back (backup) plan in the event of catastrophic conversion failure.

Developing external interfaces. Design, construct, and test all functions required to interface with external data and application resources as required in support of the optimal solutions.

Preparing for production turnover. Prepare production or operational turnover documentation and operational procedures in accordance with existing enterprise standards for operational systems.

Installing and integrating technology. Coordinate the installation, integration, and testing of any new workstation, software, server, or network technologies required to implement the optimal solutions.

Solution Implementation

Process reengineering

The solution implementation stage of the process reengineering leg deals with training users, validating data conversion efforts, and implementing process and workflow changes. This stage consists of three primary activities.

Training. Initiate and complete all formal training. On system cutover, begin intensive mentoring activities and monitor user acceptance and performance.

Validating conversion. Validate that data was converted correctly and in accordance with the timing and synchronization requirements.

System development

The solution implementation stage of the systems development leg deals with execution of the migration plan as specified and immediate response to bugs, problems, or other nonconformances associated with the system. This stage consists of four primary activities.

Installing the application. The first step is installation of the application and database within the production environment in accordance with the specifications determined by the architectural leg.

Initiating conversion. Begin execution of the data conversion functions. Monitor progress, performance, and completion of conversion process. Verify completion of the conversion process.

Deactivating old application. Depending on the nature of the conversion plan, either deactivate or isolate the old application being replaced by the new application.

Initiating operational turnover. On official acceptance by user constituency and evidence of continued application stability, initiate the procedures that turn over operational control of the application in accordance with enterprise standards and procedures.

Architecture

The solution implementation stage of the architectural leg deals with monitoring performance under actual operational conditions of both the application and its delivery foundations. This stage consists of two primary activities.

Monitoring network performance.   Closely monitor network traffic under true operational load to determine and verify that experienced work load, traffic, and performance are within original benchmark projections. Call significant variances to the immediate attention of network management and ensure that corrective actions are taken.

Monitoring data retrieval performance.   Closely monitor server performance metrics and total response time against expectations for control queries during normal system operation. Ensure that serious nonconformance with projections are immediately investigated, causes determined, and corrective action taken.

Continuous Improvement

Although this phase is often ignored or relegated to the "maintenance programmer" in traditional methodologies, it is actually the most important period in a system's life cycle. It is after the application is in production and in continual use that the enhancements begin to successively refine and extend the application's functionality as the users become more comfortable with its capabilities and the process reengineering changes begin to take hold in the daily operations. It is often the case that as much as 75 percent of a successfully introduced application's value to an organization is added in the 12 to 18 months following its implementation. It is for this reason that the continuous-improvement stage be accorded as much importance as the earlier stages of the cycle.

Process reengineering

The continuous-improvement stage of the process reengineering leg deals with gathering performance metrics and verifying that the results expected are received. Where variances from expectations exist, the team determines why and initiate corrective action as required. Once conformance with expectations has been verified, the team returns to the original problems, selecting one or more that were not quite important enough to be addressed in the original stages. The team then recycles through the same solution determination steps and initiates efforts to extend the system's functionality to address new problems.

System development

The continuous-improvement stage of the systems development leg deals with routinely monitoring and optimizing application performance, quickly addressing nonconformances when they appear, and supporting process engineering in their continuous-improvement efforts. This often encompasses more prototyping, construction, testing, and implementation of extended functionality.

Architecture

The continuous improvement stage of the architecture leg deals with routinely monitoring and optimizing network and database performance, quickly addressing nonconformances when they appear, and supporting both process engineering and systems development in their continuous-improvement efforts. It often involves the evaluation, selection, and introduction of new technologies especially in manufacturing environments as new generations of process control and data gathering technologies are released.

Summary

Client/server technologies, in conjunction with methodologies and approaches that incorporate modern organizational approaches to quality management and continuous improvement, provide the opportunity to MIS to radically restructure the way in which it provides services to the enterprise and to actually become the business partner it professes to be. On the other hand, you will not be able to realize the full benefit of the technologies if you attempt to apply them using the same outmoded approaches of the past.

You might have noticed that the discussion of the methodology was primarily about process and made no mention of specific tools or techniques. This was by design as it is my personal belief that any methodology is about process and should be flexible enough to incorporate both existing and new techniques and tools as they arise. But tools and techniques are an important part of the execution of any methodology, and it is for this reason that the next several chapters provide an overview of techniques and tools that I have found to be useful when addressing different aspects of the development process. These overviews are not meant to provide in-depth instruction in the use of these techniques but only survey an overview of what is available and has proved useful.

12

Reengineering
Tools and Techniques

This chapter identifies a number of tools and techniques, some traditionally considered specific to systems development methodologies and some not, that have proven useful in the analysis of process, determination of problems, and identification of solutions. As such these are uniquely well suited for use in the process reengineering leg of a project.

Data-Flow Analysis

The technique of data-flow analysis was introduced in 1978 by Tom DeMarco and subsequently enhanced and expanded into fully specified methodologies by a number of others, most notably Chris Gane and Trish Sarson. This technique attempts to understand the problem space being addressed by identification of the basic processes taking place within that space and analysis of the flow of data from process to process. The basic graphic mechanism by which this understanding is communicated is known as a *data-flow diagram* (DFD).

As illustrated in Fig. 12.1, and explained in greater detail below, the DFD attempts to define an operational problem space by modeling the processes, data flows between processes, data stores, and entities external to, but interacting with, the problem space.

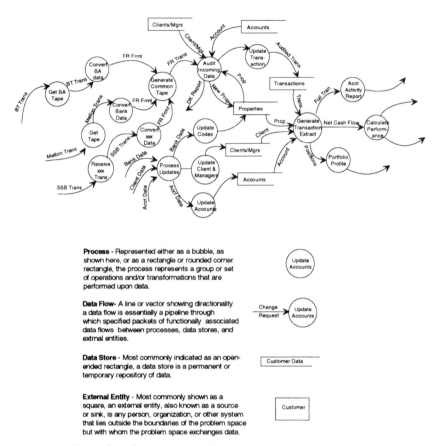

Process - Represented either as a bubble, as shown here, or as a rectangle or rounded corner rectangle, the process represents a group or set of operations and/or transformations that are performed upon data.

Data Flow- A line or vector showing directionality a data flow is essentially a pipeline through which specified packets of functionally associated data flows between processes, data stores, and extrnal entities.

Data Store - Most commonly indicated as an open-ended rectangle, a data store is a permanent or temporary repository of data.

External Entity - Most commonly shown as a square, an external entity, also known as a source or sink, is any person, organization, or other system that lies outside the boundaries of the problem space but with whom the problem space exchanges data.

Figure 12.1   Data-flow diagram notation.

Although originally developed to model the complex data interactions between system processes, the data-flow diagram is also an excellent technique for process analysis and is an effective way for both the user and the analyst to communicate their understanding of the processes within the defined problem space. This also provides an excellent tool for identifying process "problems" and modeling potential solutions to those problems. Unfortunately, the technique has a number of weaknesses when its use is extended beyond problem analysis to usage throughout the system design life cycle.

The DFD can rapidly grow beyond comprehension when modeling any sizable problem space. Although functional decomposition of each process into lower-level diagrams helps abstract this detail, the boundaries of the decomposition often tend to be highly subjective and meaningless to any but the analyst who drew the diagram. Because the DFD models process, it tends to become out-of-date very quickly as processes in today's organizations have a tendency to change frequently to meet the operational pressures of decreased resources, increased demand, and increasing competition.

The DFD technique's greatest weakness, though, is its emphasis on process to the exclusion of analysis of the data itself to determine the data's inherent structure. This is an especially serious flaw in terms of today's on-line database systems. When the principles of the DFD were being formulated the typical information system was made up of a group of batch programs executing in a linear manner, passing "files" from one program to another from beginning to end. In this type of system data does appear to "flow" from one process to another in a manner equivalent to the DFD. In modern interactive database systems data tends not to "flow" from process to process but, instead, changes its state in place as it is acted on by external events. This is a fundamental change that serves to invalidate the DFD approach for systems design, although it is still a valuable tool for performing process analysis.

Workflow Analysis

The reengineering process is essentially one of examination of current activities in terms of how work flows through a typical operational problem space. This examination is done with the intent of identifying significant bottlenecks, disconnects between related activities, and unnecessary or redundant steps that become candidates for deletion. Workflow analysis is a discipline that, unlike data-flow analysis, is targeted specifically at analysis of the actual work being performed in terms of the interactions between people within the problem space. A number of techniques and tools have begun to appear that aid in the application of this discipline. ActionWork Analysis, a copyrighted workflow analysis technique and methodology from Action Technologies, Inc, is one of the more fully defined and useful. Based on the work of Fernando Flores of Business

Design Associates and Raul Medina-Mora, Terry Winograd, Rodrigo Flores, and others at Action Technologies, Inc, ActionWork Analysis models a problem space in terms of the work-related activity-based interactions between people within the problem space, represented as a workflow diagram that graphically depicts a group of associated workflow loops.

The basic atomic element of the workflow diagram is the workflow loop. Illustrated in Fig. 12.2, the workflow loop encapsulates such interactions as a cyclic set of communications between a "customer" requesting a service and a "performer" providing the service. As shown above, each workflow loop consists of four phases:

- *Propose*—the stage of a workflow where the "customer" requests a service and specifies the conditions that must be met for the provision of that service to be satisfactory.

- *Agreement*—the stage where the "customer" and the "performer" agree on the terms of satisfaction, the cycle time of the performance of the activity, and any unusual conditions pertaining to the service.

- *Performance*—the stage where the actual work necessary to deliver the requested service is performed. It is from this stage that "work" flows out to additional subworkflows for completion and then back to the exit point of this stage.

- *Satisfaction*—the stage dealing with the delivery of the service to the customer and acceptance by the customer of that service.

The elements of a workflow diagram, as illustrated in Fig. 12.3, can be combined to model workflow processes of great complexity and serve as a very useful tool in the analysis and

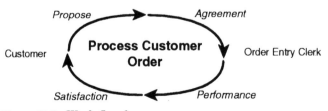

Figure 12.2 Work flow loop.

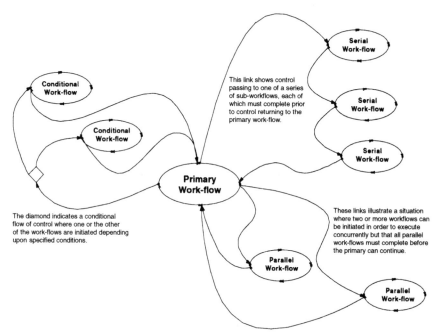

Figure 12.3   Workflow notation.

optimization of reliable processes within the problem space being addressed.

Cause-and-Effect Diagrams

As illustrated in Fig. 12.4, cause-and-effect diagrams are an effective graphical aid in the identification and classification of problems and their causes. These assist in the efforts to systematically

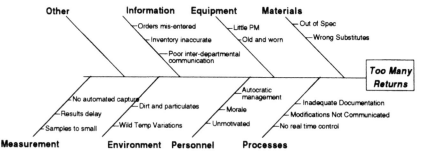

Figure 12.4   Cause/effect diagram.

gather and organize people's thoughts on the potential causes of a problem and provide a framework in which further discussion of these causes can be structured in an optimal manner.

This technique serves to enhance communication between members of the work team. It further acts as a useful mechanism to focus peoples' attention on the most probable causes of a particular undesirable effect and makes it far easier to initially identify those "causes" about which something can be done and those which are outside the work team's authority to address. Cause-and-effect diagrams tend to prevent "tunnel vision" and serve to expand the work team's thinking beyond the obvious by encouraging the identification of as many potential causes as possible. Finally, and most importantly, the cause-and-effect diagram provides a framework within which more information can be gathered to further quantify "how" a specific cause contributes to an effect, and promotes the discovery of alternatives to measure the impact of a specific cause.

Brainstorming

Brainstorming is primarily a communication technique that is admirably suited to the rapid identification of options and alternatives. It basically operates on the principle that the more ideas and proposals available, the greater the likelihood that one or more of those are going to be useful and worthy of further development. Brainstorming, as a free-wheeling intellectual and communicative activity, can easily get out of control and waste both energy and time of the participants if the sessions are not structured and monitored in a manner that promotes focused activity. Some guidelines to facilitating this focus are

- Clearly state the purpose and objective of each brainstorming session before beginning.
- Encourage the free-wheeling identification and promotion of "wild" ideas. Don't try to limit ideas to only those that are "feasible" or "tried and true."
- Generate as many ideas as possible. Be more concerned about quantity than quality. The more ideas generated, the greater the probability that good ones will surface.

- Ensure that everyone participates. No one can sit on the side-lines in a brainstorming session. Consider setting minimum goals for how many ideas each person has to contribute or awarding some form of reward or recognition for people with the greatest number of proposals.

- Never criticize an idea during initial identification. This tends to inhibit people from sharing their ideas.

- Structure and schedule each session so that it builds on the successes of the previous ones, retaining potentially good ideas, expanding them, testing them, and modifying them to fit. Stress that all ideas are the work team's ideas, no particular individual's. Modification of your ideas or other ideas is great as it ultimately leads to higher quality solutions. There should be no pride of ownership or any ego invested in any specific idea.

Rapid Prototyping

Rapid prototyping refers to a technique that has proved to be invaluable in the capturing and specification of requirements. Further, the flexibility and ease of use of client/server technologies will make it easier than it has ever been to implement this technique as a integral part of the development process. Rapid prototyping begins with the first approximations of the business solutions being addressed in the reengineering leg of the project. As soon as an early information model identifying the various data objects has been developed and the areas of human/system interface identified, rapid prototyping can begin with early models of the alternative user interfaces being considered. The task is usually addressed through small focused user meetings and interviews that introduce the initial prototype and solicit suggestions for its improvement and extension. Iteration of the changes is begun with daily meetings of the focus group to successively refine user interface, gather new requirements, and modify previously specified requirements as the users' perception of what they want changed after seeing what they can get. Initiate inclusive weekly meetings with the full project team to review progress and discuss the week's changes. Continue this process until the users are satisfied that the prototype demonstrates all essential user needs and that the information model is complete. Primary objective is speed and high interactivity with the end user with the goal of being able to deliver a functioning prototype that demonstrates all essential user interactive requirements and a rigorously documented set of nondemonstratable requirements that include specification for nontrivial, complex, or algorithmically complicated processes within 6 to 8 weeks from initiation of the process.

Chapter

13

Data Analysis

This chapter focuses on tools, techniques, and methods that have proved effective for analyzing the use of information within an enterprise. In today's typical application development efforts, data analysis is playing an increasingly important role and is a critical step in the development of enterprise-oriented applications. Traditionally, applications were often viewed as stand-alone, independent processes that were designed and built to meet the needs of a specific department or other organizational unit. As businesses became larger and more sophisticated, the information itself, apart from the application, began to be viewed as a critically important asset. Further, as these enterprises sought to integrate their operations and reengineer their basic operational processes, they found that the widespread proliferation of redundant, unsynchronized, and essentially uncontrolled data in use across the various applications represented a serious obstacle to achieving enterprise goals. Consequently, enterprises are now focusing on large systems of applications that integrate the usage of shared, nonredundant, and controlled enterprise-wide repositories of mission-critical information.

Information modeling is the primary technique in use today to capture the essential nature of how information is used and should be structured in order to support an enterprise's business goals. Information modeling is the process of identifying, inventorying, organizing, and quantifying the information used by an organization and as such represents the public lexicon of the shared information resources of an enterprise. The information model captures and presents a context within which information can be analyzed at a higher level, and apart from, specific business applications, and its primary purpose is to classify and organize the enterprise's institutional memory.

Information Modeling

Information modeling is a technique that grew out of efforts to apply a rigorous approach to designing databases in accordance with the "natural" structure of the data being stored. The intent of the information model is to define the problem space being analyzed in terms of the information contained within that problem space. This information is defined through three primary constructs: the entity, the attribute, and the relationship. An entity is a "thing" about which information needs to be tracked and maintained. An attribute specifies the information to be tracked about a specific entity type. A relationship is a link between two entities that serves to model an association between instances of these related entity types that are perceived by the end user as existing within the problem space. The information model is generally described in terms of an entity relationship diagram, as illustrated in Fig. 13.1.

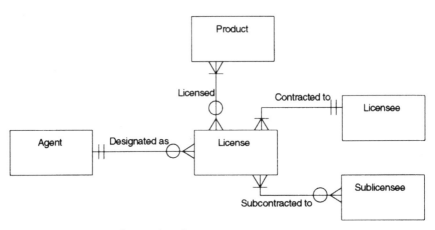

Figure 13.1   Entity relationship diagram.

Notation and terminology

Although a variety of differing notational standards have evolved since entity relationship diagrams were first introduced in the early 1980s, the basic diagramming principles, components, and techniques are essentially unchanged, and Fig. 13.2 illustrates one of the more popular notational styles.

Entity - Something about which there exists a need to store and maintain information.

Cardinality - Defined as the minimum and maximum number of occurrences of instances of relationship that are possible between two entity types.

Relationship Entity - A special type of relationship which has attributes of its own that serve to specify in greater detail the relationship between two other entities.

Multi-typing - A type of relationship between entities that models a super-class / sub-class association. For example an item can be sub-typed as both a Part or a Product.

Inclusive/Exclusive - The sub-types can optionally be indicated as a filled circle (exclusive) or unfilled circle (inclusive) as required.

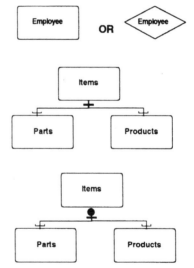

Recursion - A relationship between two occurrences of the same entity type. Most often found in bill of material type structures but also used any time there is a need to model an N-ary hierarchical relationship of the same entity type.

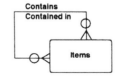

Figure 13.2 E/R notation.

Heuristics

Much of the difficulty in information modeling, at whatever level, is semantic. Attempting to identify and separate valid entities, attributes, and relationships is often difficult. The following rules of thumb are offered as guidelines to aid in this activity.

Entity. A valid entity must have an attribute or combination of attributes that can be used to uniquely identify every instance of that entity. A valid entity must also have, in addition to its unique identifiers, at least one other attribute that serves to describe the entity. Entities often equate to nouns in a specification.

Associative entity. An associative entity must be fully dependent, for its existence, on each of the other two entities to which it is related. Further, in addition to the combination of each of the associated entities' unique identifiers which, in combination, uniquely identifies the associative entity, at least one other attribute that goes to describe the associative entity must be tracked.

Attribute. An attribute must be able to be expressed in terms of a specific domain of valid values and be valid for every instance of the entity type for which it is a descriptive characteristic.

Multityping. If only a subset of instances of a given entity type can participate in a given relationship, or if all the attributes used to describe an entity are not universally applicable across all instances of that entity, or if an entity type may be two or more "things" (i.e., a part can be both a component assembly and a product) at the same time, consider multityping the entity into subtypes broken along lines of common attributes or uncommon relationships.

Reasonability. It is highly unlikely that an entity not be related to at least one other entity in a problem space. Any stand alone entity should definitely be viewed with suspicion.

As illustrated in Fig. 13.3, information modeling proceeds through three stages beginning with a conceptual model that identifies the primary business objects (i.e., entities and/or attributes) and maps their relationships within the problem

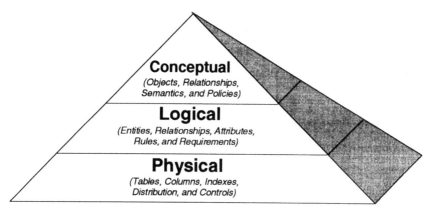

Figure 13.3 Information model levels.

space. Following the conceptual model, a logical model is developed that identifies and specifies the attributes that characterize each entity and relationship-entity, resolve super/subclassing issues, determine the unique keys and foreign keys that establish the relationships, determine domains of valid values for the attributes, and uncover organization specific policies governing the usage of the information being modeled.

The final stage is the transition of the logical model into a physical database design. This process maps the logical model to a specific physical database schema, effecting transition of entities to tables, attributes to field data types, and domain and policy constraints to appropriate database mechanisms, and making the types of design compromises necessary to ensure efficient storage and access to the data being stored. The remainder of this chapter will outline the process through which these stages are generally completed.

The Conceptual Model

The conceptual model is essentially a tool for coping with complexity. In any enterprise of significant size the total number of identifiable entities (things about which information is captured and retained) that are dealt with throughout the enterprise will run into the thousands. The number of relationships amongst these entities will be an order of magnitude greater, as will attributes. People have great difficulty dealing with that amount of detail, and it is necessary to abstract out of that detail, from the top down or bottom up, the essential core of the information, and this is the primary purpose of the conceptual model.

Step 1: identify objects

This is the process of identifying as many of the primary information objects as can be recognized within the problem space. Information objects are essentially anything that appears to be associated with data and will typically include "things" that will later be classified as either entities, attributes, or relationships. At this stage you are not concerned with classification but with recovery. Typical sources for recovering this information are meeting notes, requirements documents, written procedures, existing systems, conversations with users and analysts, meetings, personal knowledge, and any other forms of communication associated with the project. Almost all nouns are prime candidates for objects.

As each object is identified, record its existence and capture at least a business description of the object and its purpose. Data dictionaries, design repositories, and case tools all offer ideal places for storing this information, but even a simple spreadsheet will suffice.

Step 2: classify objects

Make initial determination as to whether the object is an entity, an attribute, or a relationship. Establish both ends of the identified relationships. Associate any attributes identified with existing entities. Any attributes that cannot be associated with an existing entity imply the existence of an as-yet unknown entity. Seek out and identify. Basic heuristics that serve to guide this effort are:

- If the verbal description appears to indicate that the object is described by a number of characteristics, it is probably an entity.

- If it has an attribute that appears to uniquely identify each occurrence of the object, it is probably an entity.

- If the business needs to retain information about individual instances of the object, it is probably an entity.

- If it is a compound noun phrase, then it is likely that a relationship or relationship entity linking two other entities is being identified. For example, "customer product information" may imply that there is an entity "customer," an entity "product" (your company's), and a relationship between the two, "customer product," about which is stored customer-specific information concerning a product.

- If it is multivalued, it is probably an entity. For example, "customer address" may appear to be an attribute until you discover a customer can have many addresses.

- If it is single-valued, it is probably an attribute. For example, "customer name" can have only a single value associated with it for a single occurrence of "customer."

- If it is single-valued and definitely an attribute but the qualifying noun has not yet been identified as an object then that noun represents an entity. For example, "purchase order number" implies the existence of an entity called "purchase order."

- If the context of the description contains a verb or verb form, it is probably a relationship. For example, "customers place orders" identifies a relationship between a customer entity and an order entity.

- If attributes of two separate entities appear in close proximity in some form of user view (screen, report, etc.), then there is a relationship between those entities.

- If the description of an attribute mentions more than one entity, then that attribute probably belongs to a relationship-entity linking the two other entities.

Step 3: quantify entities and relationships

For every entity and relationship identified, complete, at a minimum, the following information:

Business purpose. Document description of the entity and its business purpose. Determine whether it is a transient or permanent entity. Permanent entities are things about which the enterprise wishes to retain information over time. For example, "customer" would be a permanent entity. Transient entities are those about which the enterprise does not retain information over time. An example might be "customer purchase order." Although referenced over and over again, it may be determined that the enterprise is not interested in any of the customer purchase order information, with the exception of a purchase order number, once an order is taken.

Synonyms.   Document all the various synonyms by which this entity is known. One of the by-products of an effective modeling effort is to standardize the semantics and taxonomy of an enterprise's data objects. (*Caution:* Many seeming synonyms will, on reflection, often turn out to be distinct entity subtypes and therefore new entities.)

Associated attributes.   List all attributes that are known characteristics of this entity. Identify that attribute or collection of attributes that serve to uniquely identify the entity.

Identifying source.   Where was the entity identified? Where did the description and purpose come from?

Determining ownership.   What organizational unit(s) have control over the specification of this entity?

Uncovering policies.   What enterprise policies govern the usage of this entity? Who determines what those rules are?

Determining cardinality.   For every relationship identified, define its cardinality and the business events under which they come into existence and are deleted.

Step 4: quantify classification schemes

This is the first step in the process abstraction. Abstraction is important because it allows you to hide the detail in order to gain greater understanding and to plan the subsequent steps of detail analysis. It is essentially the process of grouping a bunch of trees into a far smaller group of forests, thereby allowing you to see the forest. This process begins with grouping your entities according to the nature of the associations between them. For example, the entities customer, customer contact, address, customer account are all obviously closely related. The same could be said for entities such as product, part, bill of material, inventory, specification, and work order. The intent is to derive or abstract higher-level "classes" of information expressed as groups of entities. Be aware that this can often be a highly subjective process, and as analysis proceeds you will find yourself moving entities from one class to another or even creating new classes.

The end result of this exercise, as illustrated in Figs. 13.4 and 13.5, is a smaller number of key data classes on which you can then focus your attention for more detailed analysis in the development of the logical model.

Step 5: validate

The last step in the conceptual modeling effort is validation, with the business users of the data, of the conceptual model. The objective is to ensure that all essential entities have been identified, that they have been described correctly, and that all relationships between these entities have been captured and correctly identified.

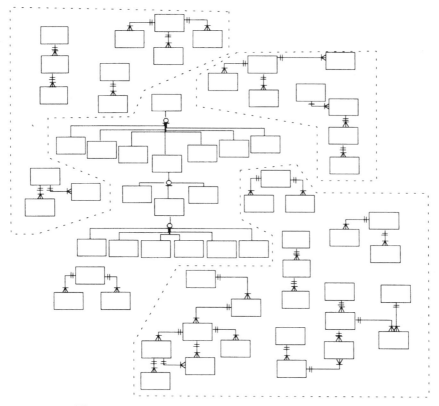

Figure 13.4 The conceptual model.

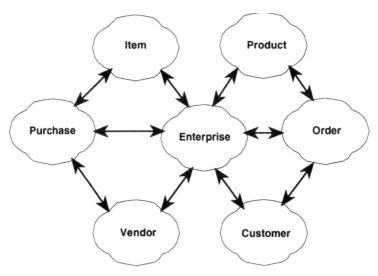

Figure 13.5   Entity classes.

The Logical Model

The next stage in the information modeling effort is the development of a logical model. The logical modeling effort is essentially an extension of the conceptual model where the purpose is to add detail, uncover remaining attributes and complete specification of all attributes, determine classification criteria where appropriate, and identify appropriate control domains. The best way to address this activity is to select an entity class and focus on fully specifying that class and completing the specification of all entities, attributes, and relationships. As new entities are identified, determine their class and begin their attribution. As a rule of thumb you can generally expect to double and possibly triple the number of entities identified in the conceptual model. The following steps are applied to each class and, within each class, these steps are iterative in nature.

Step 1: discover new entities, attributes, and relationships

The conceptual model identified all or most of the key entities. Now that you are focused on a subset of those, your task is to drill down into greater detail and discover the lower-level, less critically important, or hidden entities. This is best done in close cooperation with the reengineering leg of the project and through direct personal communication with knowledgeable users. Existing systems, if any, are good sources of new entities. As each new entity, attribute, and relationship is discovered, specify it as fully as possible. Another place within the model that new entities may be lurking is the existence of any direct many-to-many relationships between two entities. Examine these relationships with care and determine whether they have additional, as yet undiscovered, attributes that serve to define the represented intersection in greater detail. If so, and it is rare if they do not, add new relationship-entities as required.

Step 2: complete attribution

For every attribute identified, the attribute's format, length, and allowable values must be identified. Identify the conditions under which the attribute can be null and define any rules that govern the attribute's allowable values in relationship to any other attributes associated with that entity. Note all attributes that are derivable, computable, or defaultable and the conditions under which these conditions may apply. Identify all attributes that serve to "classify", and attributes with "code," "type," "kind," "category," or similar in their names are generally those used by the enterprise or smaller groups within the enterprise to classify instances of this entity for support of some business need. Examples of such classification attributes include "product code," "customer type," and "equipment class."

Step 3: quantify classification schemes

Those attributes identified as classifiers generally imply the existence of subtyping instances that you may not have yet identified. Examine each to determine whether it defines a number of subtypes and, if it does, determine the nature of the classification hierarchy and whether the subtyping is such that it governs whether certain attributes and/or relationships are limited by these types.

Step 4: identify domain control entities

For each classification attribute and such others that may have a large number of allowable values, determine whether a new entity is required to maintain and control the domain that governs that attribute's allowable values. If so, add that domain as an entity, define its attributes, and establish who in the enterprise will be the owner of that domain.

Step 5: generalize

Look for opportunities to generalize multiple entity types that appear to be very similar in nature and attribution into a single common entity that may or may not need to be subtyped. Often entities that appear to be separate and distinct are actually roles being played by a higher-level entity in relationship with the enterprise itself. Examine entities such as customer and vendor or sales representative and manager. Are many of the same attributes being captured for each? Are the relationships established similar in scope and purpose? Does the enterprise tend to establish multiple different relationships with instances of the entity type? For example, vendor and customer may both be just roles played with the enterprise by a higher-level entity called "company." "Sales representative" and "manager" may both be roles played by an entity type called "employee."

Step 6: validate

The last step in the logical modeling effort, as also applies for the conceptual model, is validation, with the business users of the data, of the expanded and more fully specified logical model. The objective is to ensure that all essential entities have been identified, that they have been described correctly, that all relationships between these entities have been captured and correctly identified, that all attributes have been captured and fully specified, and that the ownership of all domains is correctly documented.

The Physical Model

The next stage in the information modeling effort is the development of a physical database design. As such this stage is concerned with transforming the logical model into a physical model that can be implemented in the database management system being used. This stage is essentially one of compromise where the "pure" models derived from conceptual and logical analysis are "corrupted" in order to optimize access to the data in the "real world." Prototyping and benchmarking should play a big role in the development of the physical model, and my recommendation is that this be considered an iterative process that begins with the logical model as is.

Step 1: implement logical model

This step entails coding whatever structures are necessary within the given DBMS to implement the fully specified logical model as it is defined. Once the schema is established, the database is populated in accordance with expectations. If migration of legacy data will be effected, it is done for the first time at this point. If no data is available to populate the database, a set of "dummy" data will be created that statistically models the expected characteristics of the expected population, and that dummy data will then be loaded. Initial candidates for indexes will be identified (primary keys, foreign keys, etc.) and appropriate index types (hashed, clustered, etc.) selected, coded, and established.

Step 2: benchmark

This step entails taking the access patterns being defined by the prototyping and requirement definition activities, coding them against the current schema, and analyzing the access plans produced by the DBMS on the queries' submissions. Alternative index strategies are tried until query performance no longer continues to improve.

Step 3: design adjustments

This step deals with analysis of the physical schema for opportunities to increase query performance. Quite often the design goal at this point is to reduce join requirements. Opportunities are examined that meet this need. Examples include analysis of the subtyping relationships among entities for "compressing" a potentially multilevel subtyped hierarchy into a single table, introducing planned key or attribute redundancy into "child" or dependent attributes to reduce the need for joins with the parent, or consolidation of multiple different domain tables (if attributes share common formats) into a single table. New indexes are introduced where necessary to take advantage of the adjustments. Benchmarks are executed again to validate the access patterns and verify the improvements made, if any. This is a highly iterative process that continues until the physical model has been optimized as much as deemed prudent.

Step 4: analyze impact on update processing

The types of design adjustments that take place in step 3 often have the potential for severely impacting the performance of update processing. Adding indexes, introducing redundancy, and other similar adjustments all tend to degrade data maintenance performance. Depending on the nature of the application (high-volume transaction processing vs. decision support, etc.), this can be of greater or lesser concern to the database designer, and an optimal balance that meets the needs of the application must be achieved. Once again, benchmarking is the primary tool used to determine the impact, identifying new adjustment, and verifying whether optimal performance is being achieved.

Step 5: determine data placement strategy

This is the final step in the optimization model and attempts to achieve further optimization through intelligently distributing the data across multiple controller channels and multiple drive devices in order to balance the server's I/O throughput and achieve the highest level of throughput concurrency as is possible given the physical limitations of the server platform.

Step 6: design and implement control mechanisms

Depending on the DBMS technology being used, a significant amount of the access, integrity, and domain control logic of the application may be embedded in the database itself. Those mechanisms that are targeted for embedding in the database are now designed in accordance with the rules defined in conceptual and logical modeling against an optimized and stable physical model. Additional mechanisms are added to ensure that all redundancy introduced by the optimization process is controlled by additional logic at the database level. The final step in this process is to implement those security features that control access to the final database in accordance with the requirements defined in conceptual and logical modeling.

Summary

As I think you can see, the greatest strengths of the information modeling technique are its simplicity and its applicability across the entire scope of project's cycle. Information modeling maps very closely to the normal manner in which people perceive their environment and is easily understood by end users. Further, the information model is based on an understanding of the problem space, which will tend to be very stable, unlike that in data-flow analysis. The weakness of information modeling is that, like data-flow analysis, its perception of the problem space tends to be one-dimensional, focused only on the data itself, and makes no effort to detect or model the changing "states" of the entities and relationships once modeled. This static view of the problem space tends to ignore the manner in which events occurring in the problem space interact with information within that problem space. Like data-flow analysis, information modeling describes only half of the problem.

14

Architectural Design

The basic problem in application architecture design is the intangibility of software. You can't see it, feel it, touch it, or taste it, and this makes it supremely difficult to "architect" a design and communicate this design to those tasked with building it. Add to this the fact that truly large software projects represent some of the most complex constructs ever built. The primary tools to aid in this process therefore have to address this "visualization" problem in a manner that adds specificity and removes ambiguity. These aids fulfill the same function as a blueprint does for an architect designing a building that a contractor will be building. This chapter discusses two such tools that have proved useful in this visualization and architectural specification process.

Structure Chart

The structure chart diagram is another useful technique that came out of Tom DeMarco's work in structured analysis and design theory. The structure chart, as illustrated in Fig. 14.1, is a graphical approach to defining both the logical (using functions) and physical (using modules) structure of a system in terms of a hierarchical network of interrelated boxes. As a physical system design tool, the structure chart performs much the same purpose as Mr. Booch's module and process diagrams.

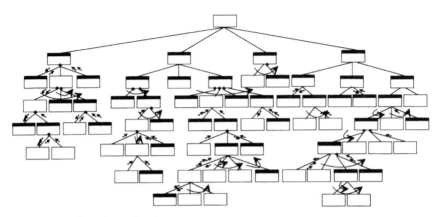

Figure 14.1   Structure chart.

As shown in Fig. 14.2, the notation is very simple and straightforward.

Once a logical structure chart is developed by decomposition of a system's functions, a physical structure chart is developed to package the logical functions into physical subsystems, programs, and modules based on four well-defined principles which are as valid today for client/server applications as they were 15 years ago for the design of mainframe systems.

Coupling

An analysis of the couples that exist between two functions is performed to determine how interdependent the functions actually are. The more "data" being passed between the functions, the more tightly coupled they are said to be, while "control" information being passed indicates looser coupling. The more tightly coupled two functions are, the more likely they should be encapsulated into one module.

Cohesion

This is a measure of the strength between the elements within two coupled functions. If the functions are highly dependent on the internal processing or logical paths of one or the other, then they are highly cohesive and should be encapsulated into a single module.

Function - A "black box" representation of a process defined at the level of abstraction appropriate to its position in the hierarchy of such functions that make up a design.

Connection - A vector that joins two modules representing a passing of control from one module to another The hierarchical nature of a structure chart implies such passing of control is generally in a top down, left to right sequence.

Couple - An arrow with a tail that graphically depicts the direction and movement of data or control switches between functions.

Iteration - A curved line indicates iteration or "looping" through the sequence of "functions" included within the loop. Multiple concentric lines indicate loops within loops from the inside out.

Decision - A diamond indicates a decision point or branch that determines either an exclusive(or) or inclusive (and/or) branch between two or more lower level functions.

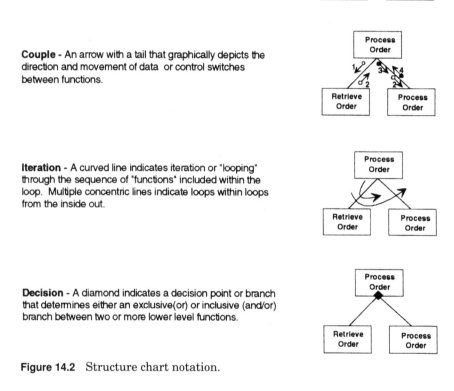

Figure 14.2   Structure chart notation.

Span of control

This is a measure of the control that one function exerts over other subordinate functions. Functions whose internal processing is strongly controlled by the logical decisions made within another function should be encapsulated together into a module.

Scope of effect

This is a measure of the impact of the logical decisions of one function over the optional execution or nonexecution of other functions. Generally speaking, a module should encapsulate all lower-level functions which will be strongly influenced by the decision paths within a higher-level function.

Rapid Prototyping

Rapid prototyping is a technique that has come into widespread acceptance as an approach to gathering requirements that is faster, more effective, and better suited to today's client/server technologies than the more traditional structured analysis and design techniques. It stresses highly interactive sessions between the ultimate users and the system designer where iterative attempts to design trial versions of a system are modeled, modified, and continuously improved until a full understanding of the needs and requirements of the user is attained by the system designer and a clear visualization of the final product is achieved by the ultimate user. The resulting prototype reflects the real requirements far more accurately than traditional specification methods and additionally provides a foundation on which to develop a fully functional production-grade application.

Rapid prototyping is not constrained to any specific formal theories, techniques, or tools but is, instead, a framework or methodology, as illustrated in Fig. 14.3, within which the developer can choose and apply data-flow analysis, information modeling, and object-oriented analysis and design tools as needed to address specific needs throughout the project life cycle. As an approach to systems development, rapid prototyping is uniquely well suited to the characteristics of the client/server environment.

Object-Oriented Analysis and Design

Object-oriented analysis, design, and programming (OOA, OOD, OOP) are a relatively new and still somewhat immature set of techniques to aid in the analysis, design, and development of information systems. Object orientation builds on many of the concepts of information modeling, extending the defini-

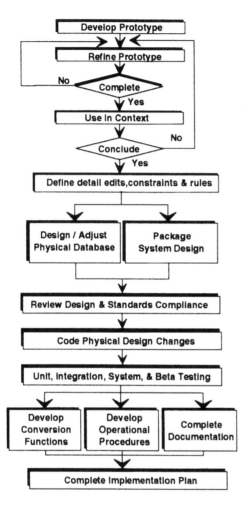

Figure 14.3   Typical prototyping work flow.

tion and description of entities to include the services that act
on the entity. An entity with services then becomes an object
within OOA terminology. Within this model objects are organized into three basic collections: descriptive (objects + attributes), groups (classes of objects, subclasses of classes), and
assemblies (supertypes and subtypes).

The techniques go further to create and define a framework
within which objects, made up of both data and services that
act on that data, interact with one another by sending messages which are essentially a request from one object to another
for the receiving object to do something to itself. An object-ori-

ented approach to modeling, designing, and building an application applies three primary principles to the understanding of
a problem space.

Abstraction. Also a primary principle of information modeling, abstraction applies the basic human cognitive activity of
simplification by emphasizing the essential characteristics of
an object that serve to distinguish it from other objects and
hiding those characteristics that are irrelevant and serve
only to clutter the picture. Abstraction provides the view of
an object from an external perspective.

Encapsulation. Encapsulation is the principle of hiding the
details and characteristics of an object from any other objects
external to it. Encapsulation is the logical follow-on to abstraction but applied with great discipline by explicitly defining a
boundary between the object and the outside world. Encapsulation is essentially the view of an object from an internal perspective.

Inheritance. Inheritance is the principle that, in any given
set of objects and their relationships, there will occur a natural hierarchy of relationships that are parent ↔ child in
nature. In such hierarchical relationship sets certain characteristics of the higher-level objects can be "inherited" by their
lower-level descendants.

The power and flexibility of these basic concepts serve to
extend the developer's understanding of a problem space beyond
the static information model into a more fully defined and complete description of the objects existing within the boundaries of
that space, the events that occur to change the state of those
objects, and the manner in which those objects interact with one
another. Further, these inherent characteristics of object orientation as it applies to the system development process promise
significant advances in the reusability of code, higher-quality
solutions, and decreasing development time. Object orientation
is a natural and complementary extension of the client/server
architecture and uniquely suited to leveraging the strengths of
that environment. A number of development languages are
available today that implement these principles at a coding
level. Modern versions of SmallTalk, the original object-oriented

language developed at Xerox's Palo Alto Research Center, have evolved in very powerful full-function tools and are available today from vendors such as DigiTalk and ParcPlace. Tools such as C++ and Powersoft's Powerbuilder have enhanced their capabilities with extensive object-oriented facilities and new object-oriented tools are appearing almost daily.

Unfortunately, the methodologies needed to guide their usage are not yet codified to the point of being considered "standard practice." No fully defined methodologies or widely accepted graphical and notational standards yet exist to guide the application of these principles in the earlier stages of development to support analysis, requirements definition, and system design. Probably the most fully defined notational guidelines are those put forward by Grady Booch, who identifies four basic diagram types, each with its own notational standards, to address the various stages of the OOA and OOD cycle.

Each of these diagram types, as illustrated in Fig. 14.4, exist to support a specific "view" of the problem space in terms of static classification and relationships (class diagrams), dynamic interaction and changes of state (state transitions and object diagrams), modularization (module diagrams), and physical process distribution (process diagrams). As you can see, the notational approach is somewhat complex, especially in comparison to data flow, entity relationship diagrams, and structure charts. The complexity and special notation limit the usefulness of these diagrams as an end-user communication tool, although they do serve, for analysts and other technical personnel, to adequately capture the full complexity of a given problem space.

Benchmarking

The third technique of supreme usefulness to the architect doesn't aid in visualization and design but is invaluable in verification and testing. I'm referring to the process of benchmarking, but not in the sense that we have become accustomed to vendors using benchmarks as tools to market their wares against competing products. No, application benchmarking is the process of actually testing your designs and implementation under conditions as close to the expected production environ-

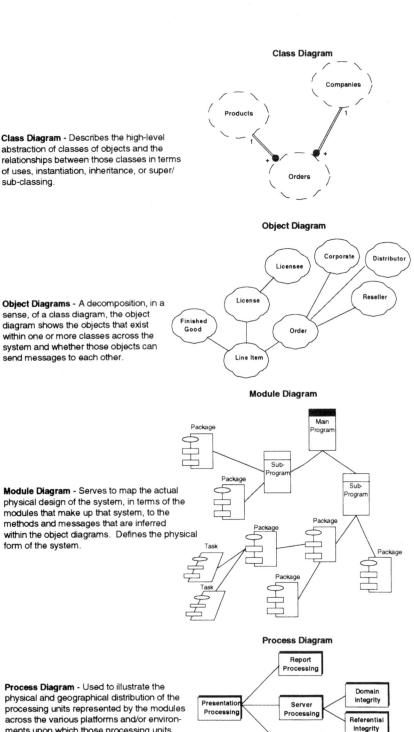

Class Diagram

Class Diagram - Describes the high-level abstraction of classes of objects and the relationships between those classes in terms of uses, instantiation, inheritance, or super/ sub-classing.

Object Diagram

Object Diagrams - A decomposition, in a sense, of a class diagram, the object diagram shows the objects that exist within one or more classes across the system and whether those objects can send messages to each other.

Module Diagram

Module Diagram - Serves to map the actual physical design of the system, in terms of the modules that make up that system, to the methods and messages that are inferred within the object diagrams. Defines the physical form of the system.

Process Diagram

Process Diagram - Used to illustrate the physical and geographical distribution of the processing units represented by the modules across the various platforms and/or environ- ments upon which those processing units will actually reside and operate.

Figure 14.4   Booch diagrams.

196

ment as can be simulated. Further, this benchmarking activity is not a one-time event but should be considered a standard ongoing activity that begins as early in the project as possible and continues throughout the application's life cycle.

The basic objectives of this benchmarking activity, especially in a client/server environment in which new technology is being added, should include the following:

Server optimization. Thoroughly exercise the database server platform with expected common transactions, dynamic queries, and other processing loads that are expected to be placed on the server in an operational environment. From this activity you should expect to achieve the following objectives:

Determine the nature of the response degradation rate as workstations are added and transaction rates increase using a single representative transaction.

Verify the server technology's capacity to handle expected throughput demands under a variety of conditions ranging from normal expected volumes up to the maximum possible "worst case" scenario. Determine response times to be expected under each simulation.

Determine the impact of both transaction dumps and database dumps on interactive response time.

Establish a performance baseline for the current physical database design in order to be able to quantify the benefit and impact of such future changes to that physical structure as the addition or deletion of indexes, consolidation of tables, introduction of planned redundancy, use of stored procedures, alternative "select" approaches, use of views, etc.

Use the information gathered to accurately and cost-effectively size the server technology to meet the business's needs.

Confirm reliability. Possibly the single most important objective of benchmarking in an open-systems environment, this objective seeks to verify, by testing through all performance and throughput ranges, that the technologies selected and installed will interact correctly and not fail. Where failure points are detected, replace with alternative technologies.

Network traffic. Measure expected file server "network" traffic impact on database transaction response time. Measure the impact on database transaction response of report routing across the network. Ensure that interconnection (bridges, routers, etc.) do not constitute performance bottlenecks, and if they do, reconfigure the network to erase them.

Development tool.   Test and verify, in terms of performance, ease of use, and functionality, the suitability of selected development tools.

Workstation configurations.   Test and verify the suitability of the recommended end-user workstation hardware and software configurations.

15

Client/Server-
Specific Design
Issues

Designing a client/server application offers a number of special challenges not normally faced by developers of mainframe-oriented multiuser applications. To realize the full benefits of the client/server architecture, the developer should leverage the architecture's flexibility to incorporate the greater potential for functional and data distribution into the fundamental design of the application.

Functional Distribution

By definition, a client/server application will operate across multiple platforms. At a minimum, that implies a server platform for the database and a client platform for the application. At this minimum level of utilization the design of the client/server application doesn't differ that greatly from its mainframe counterpart, and the physical design issues faced by both developers are primarily ones of packaging. But to take full advantage of the client/server paradigm, the developer needs to address issues of functional distribution of their application across not just the client and server platforms but across all the nodes of the network as well. The issues surrounding this functional distribution are the single greatest difference between the physical design of mainframe multiuser and client/server applications, and the greater granularity of distribution offered by the client/server paradigm is one of its greatest strengths.

To illustrate some of the issues and possibilities, let's examine a simplified order entry system incorporating on-line transaction processing, off-cycle batch update processing, scheduled and ad hoc production reports, and other typical special-purpose functionality. The simplest implementation might appear as illustrated in Fig. 15.1 with all "processing" performed on client workstations and the database server providing only basic data management select and update functionality.

The first step in functional distribution might be to move the edit input functions of the OLTP modules into the database server's domain and referential integrity enforcement mechanisms. Now, do you leave them in the client also? What are the reasons for moving them to the server? One good reason is so that they would be centrally administered and enforced across all applications and/or end-user queries. Why duplicate them on the client? Well, one reason would be to reduce network traffic (i.e., failed update + error message) by cleaning the data before sending it to the server. Another might be to give the end user more immediate feedback, on a field-by-field basis, as data is being entered.

The next distribution option that might occur is to move the sorting, grouping, and calculation functionality incorporated into the report functions onto the server by adding "order by...group by...and sum..." statements to the report "select..." statement, as illustrated in Fig. 15.2. Although most SQL devel-

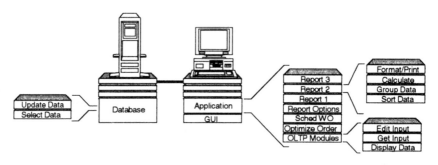

Figure 15.1 Simple distribution.

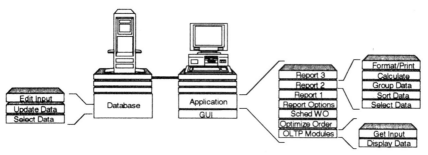

Figure 15.2   Data management distribution.

opers would automatically incorporate these into the select statement, the decision to do so should be evaluated on a case-by-case basis. If, for example, the server is heavily loaded or there is a high volume of reporting activity within the application, it might actually be more globally efficient to perform those operations on the client where only one node is affected instead of the server, where many clients might be impacted.

Another possibility, if the server is not heavily loaded and the server operating system is one conducive to application development (e.g., Unix, OS/2, Windows/NT, OS/400), is to move all the reporting functionality to the server, as illustrated in Fig. 15.3. This can be an especially effective strategy if the report does not require user interaction beyond its initiation and is always routed to a printer automatically, or if the generation of the report is scheduled to run automatically at a specific time. Although this adds to the server's processing load, it can offer several advantages that may be significant in environments where network traffic is heavy. Examine what happens when a

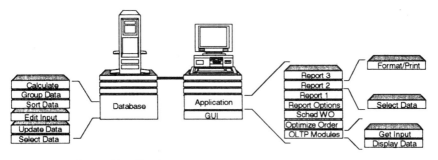

Figure 15.3   Query distribution.

client executes a report. First, the client sends the select statement to the server. Second, the server returns the result set,
which for reports will often be quite large, over the network to
the client. Third, the client processes the report and routes it,
over the network, to a network printer queue. Fourth, the network printer queue routes the report to the requested networked printer. In this scenario essentially the same data has
traveled over the wire three times, from database server to
client, client to network server, and network server to printer.
Putting the entire report function on the server reduces at least
one of these trips and, if a production printer is directly
attached to the server, the data never hits the wire at all.
Another potential advantage derived by moving the report
functions off of the client entirely is the user's ability to initiate
the report then immediately going on to something else instead
of waiting for it to complete. Even if the client is using a sophisticated multitasking operating system, it is still likely that the
user will experience some performance degradation while the
report is executing on the client.

A third alternative, illustrated in Fig. 15.4, to distributing
reporting functions where the server is not a good candidate is
to consider dedicating a client as a stand-alone report "server,"
possibly even with a dedicated directly attached high-volume

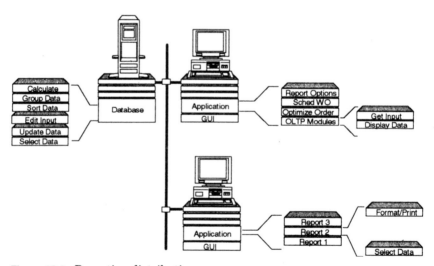

Figure 15.4 Reporting distribution.

printer. This doesn't reduce network traffic as significantly as the server option, but it does remove the processing from the initiating client and can offer administrative and management benefits as well.

Another distribution criterion that may arise in some applications is the need for special processing functionality. For example, Fig. 15.5 illustrates a situation where the order optimization function is actually a linear programming exercise of great complexity and, for reasonable responsiveness, requires heavy-duty computational support. In this scenario, that special-purpose function might be performed on a dedicated RISC (reduced instruction set computer) processor.

These rather simplistic scenarios have illustrated the types of distribution decisions that should be part of your system design process in a client/server application. At some point in the future, application development tools will no doubt appear that will make many of these decisions for you and probably implement them dynamically throughout the environment on the basis of what client and server resources are available at any given time. Until then, these are design issues that should be considered by the developer of any significant client/server application. Keeping in mind that the distribution decisions you

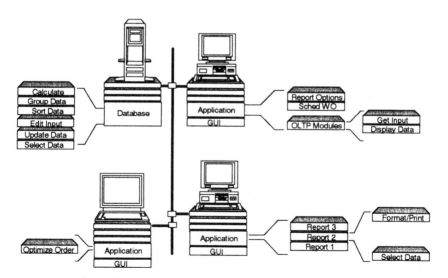

Figure 15.5 Special processing distribution.

will make will be driven by the nature of the application and the environment in which it is meant to operate, I would like to offer the following rules of thumb, which may prove useful in determining functional distribution.

- Locate the functionality as close as possible to the source of that functionality's input and target of that function's output. Where source and target are different locations, consider decomposing the functionality further.

- Locate the functionality on the platform that provides the most appropriate resources for the support of that functionality.

- Locate the functionality where it will act to conserve resources in the following priority:

Conserve shared server resources.

Conserve shared network bandwidth.

Conserve client resources.

Data Distribution

A distributed database is defined as a collection of data that is distributed across multiple different platforms that are connected by a communications network and that provides localized application access to that data in a manner that is transparent to the application. Distributed databases are not new, nor are they a consideration unique to client/server architectures or relational databases. Data distribution needs, no doubt, arose immediately after the first database management systems appeared 20 years ago, and various solutions to the distribution problem have been implemented over the years on mainframe and minicomputer platforms using a wide variety of database management software. A number of factors serve to justify the distribution of logically related data across physically separate platforms in any environment.

Capacity. Large centralized databases that are heavily used can often exceed the DASD and throughput capacity of their server platform, resulting in poor query performance and/or hardware constraints on the database's total size. Segmenting such a database into functional subsets spread across multiple platforms but logically presented to the application as a single database image reduces the demand processing and data storage requirements that are needed by each individual database platform.

Transmission media limitations. Where centralized data needs to be accessed by geographically remote processes, the primary performance constraint becomes the bandwidth of the telecommunication medium used to establish the connection. While the bandwidth of today's LAN ranges from 10 to 16 Mbits/s, the bandwidth of typical dedicated wide area network (WAN) linkages range from 9.6 kbits/s to 1.5 Mbits/s, at best only 10 percent of the typical LAN bandwidth. While new technologies such as ISDN and frame relay promise to increase this speed significantly, these are not yet widely available and, where available, are very expensive. Given these technological constraints, it is often far more cost-effective to distribute and store the data needed by a remote location at the remote location.

Availability. It may often be the case that a single database serves the needs of many different applications. For example, a company may have a single centralized customer database that is accessed, in addition to their own application-specific databases, by order entry, distribution and shipping, and accounts receivable applications. In the event the centralized customer database is damaged or becomes unavailable, all the applications needing customer information become inoperative. Replicating the data in the centralized customer database in each application-specific database provides protection against unscheduled interruption of service by removing a potential single point of failure.

Organizational structure. It may sometimes be the case that the organizational structure and operating policies of a company result in a situation where data ownership and usage naturally fall along organization boundaries with very little sharing of unit-level data but a very real need to assure consistent and common schemas and formats. In this situation a centrally controlled and managed schema is distributed across multiple platforms, each supporting an organizational unit that is responsible for the contents of that schema. The rare need for a consolidated view of all unit databases is then supported by a distributed query facility that presents the super-set of all servers as if it were one database.

Combining heterogeneous data sources. Probably the most common need driving data distribution efforts in large organizations, this scenario is less a strategy and more of a reaction to existing conditions. This scenario is the result of the fact that many large organizations have installed and used two or more different and often incompatible database management systems over the years. Although it is often a long-term goal to consolidate the data and applications from these different systems into one database, the cost and effort involved make this a drawn-out process and, in the meantime, there is often still a need to combine data from these sources and present it to the user as if it were a single database.

Now that that is said, let me make the point that there are many different ways to distribute data across a network and despite the promises of the database software vendors, the day of full and transparent data distribution is still somewhere in the future. The very nature of data distribution imposes a number of design constraints on the application architect. These constraints require detailed analysis to determine an appropriate strategy that is both in line with the enterprise's needs and implementable given the current state of the technology. Some of the more important of these constraints are:

- Location transparency for application access.
- Performance for distributed queries over wide area networks and relatively slow transmission lines.
- Fully distributed security that encompasses all servers that may provide residence to one or more "chunks" of distributed data.
- Full transaction management, distributed update commit protocols for failure detection and backout, and distributed concurrency control.
- Allowance for failures of localized resources.
- Organizational ownership of distributed data.

Data distribution takes three basic forms today with various database software vendors purporting to provide solutions at various levels of performance for each form.

Distributed update.   This form of data distribution essentially allows the data to be fully partitioned across multiple different platforms while the database engine itself takes care of ensuring that updates are distributed to the appropriate servers, as illustrated in Fig. 15.6, and ensures that full transaction management and commit and backout capability is enforced throughout the network. This is provided with full transparency as far as the application is concerned.

Distributed query.   Figure 15.7 illustrates a much less technically challenging form of distribution and essentially provides full distributed query-only transparency to the application,

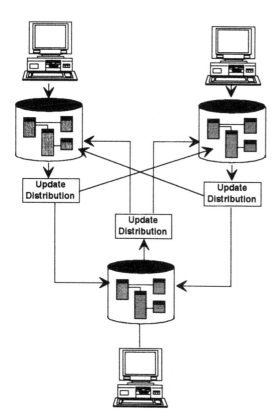

Figure 15.6 Distributed update.

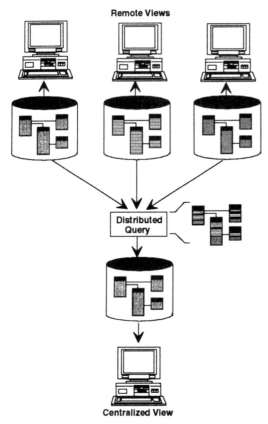

Figure 15.7 Distributed query.

with the database engine being responsible for maintaining knowledge of the data location, initiating retrieval activities including joins across distributed data resources, and presentation of the final result set to the application.

Data replication.   This is by far the simplest and least challenging of the data distribution forms and, for that reason, is often the most useful. As illustrated in Fig. 15.8, data replication is the process by which the database engine is responsible for replicating designated and selected data across multiple servers automatically in the event of a change in the state of that data. This replication takes place asynchronously and thus does not need to surmount the technical challenges of distributed updates. In the event of a problem, localization

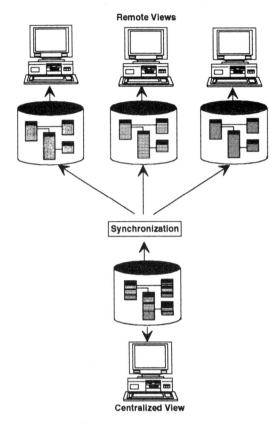

Figure 15.8   Data replication.

failure, or communication interruption, the engine just keeps trying until it succeeds in replicating the data where it was told to. Again, this is transparent to the application and is essentially a server-to-server function.

Given the technical obstacles to full distributed update capability, the performance impact of distributed queries, especially when those queries are distributed over a wide area network, and the rapidly decreasing cost and increasing capacity of server technologies, it is difficult to come up with a business justification for full real-time data distribution. Storing data redundantly across multiple platforms in order to put it physically close to the users of that data and using some form of data replication to synchronize the data resources is generally a far more cost-effective and high-performance approach that also serves to limit the impact on the enterprise of localized system failures.

The real issues that have to be addressed in your more typical everyday business applications contemplating distributing data across a network are policy in nature. Before determining the "ideal" geographic or organizational distribution of data, ensure that the following issues are addressed:

Ownership.   Who owns the definition of the data? Who controls the domains that enforce classification and categorization integrity?

Custodianship.   Who is responsible for maintaining the data? Along what lines will custodianship be defined (database, table, row, column, application, etc.)? Who is responsible for the completeness and integrity of the data over which custodianship is being exercised?

Sensitivity.   What data is sensitive with its distribution and/or access to be tightly controlled?

Security.   Who will be the "keeper of the keys"? Will security administration be distributed along with the data, or will it be centralized?

16

Futures

It is readily apparent, even to the traditional mainframe developer, that client/server architecture is the future of application development. The dynamics of the technology market, rapidly decreasing cost, and information processing needs of today's corporation can only serve to increase the pace of conversion to this approach. What is not so certain is what the client/server environment of the future will look like. As we have discussed, the very flexibility of the architecture is its greatest strength, and predicting its future direction is difficult at best. But there are a number of current trends that appear likely to continue into the future and significantly impact the application of the client/server approach to application development.

Business Needs

Over the last 30 years or so we have seen the introduction of information processing into almost every facet of the business, yet many studies indicate that the productivity of information workers, those who should be benefiting the most, shows little increase. A number of studies have indicated that, despite the increased number of centralized database applications, less than 10 percent of the information actually needed and used by a large organization is stored within the organization's database environment. Much of the remaining 90 percent represents unstructured text, pictures, and other forms of information not traditionally addressed by database applications.

Organizations are entering a period during which their efforts will be focused on reorganization of all the organization's information into repositories where it can be easily and profitably leveraged. The goal of tomorrow's applications will be to deliver that information using whatever media, format, and method is appropriate to adequately support every aspect of an organization's daily operation.

Standards

The role of the various organizations seeking to coordinate the definition of standards has grown increasingly important and will eventually prove to be the key to a truly open computing environment. The work of the ANSI, IEEE, SAG, and X-Open groups, among others, is providing a firm foundation for a truly transparent and reliable heterogeneous environment within which developers can once again focus on the business problem to be solved instead of the technologies being used. These standards bodies, in combination with market economics, will drive the industry to consensus in three key areas.

Transport protocols

A source of most of the system integration problems experienced today, the various vendor-specific and proprietary transport protocols will in all likelihood be supplanted by a standards-based TCP/IP or enhanced TCP/IP transport mechanism backed by a fully consistent and common API.

Interprocess communication protocol

A common IPC is a critical component to distributed computing across heterogeneous platforms, and the current mix of named pipes, RPCs, APPC, and proprietary transaction protocols is another very real problem in today's client/server environments. The Open Systems Foundation (OSF) and Unix International are beginning to work together on a standard framework for distributed computing environments (DCEs). Once established and implemented, market economics will drive the incorporation of these facilities into the next generation of operating systems.

SQL call-level interface

The last major obstacle to database transparency in client/ server environments is the application's interface to the database. The SQL access group's work on standardizing a common SQL call-level interface and Microsoft's and Borland's commitment to driving the implementation of the standard is already beginning to significantly simplify the developer's task, and this simplification will continue until the database implementation is truly transparent to the developer.

Object-Oriented Programming

Although still in a formative stage and not yet in widespread use, the object-oriented programming paradigm promises significant developer productivity increases, after the learning curve is ascended, and will fundamentally change the way in which systems are designed and constructed. We are already beginning to see toolkit collections from SmallTalk vendors DigiTalk and ParcPlace that point the way to a future where systems won't be built so much as they are packaged from already existing reusable objects.

Fully Distributed Processing

Combine the trends illustrated above with the rapidly increasing power and decreasing cost of workstation hardware, the increased sophistication of the next generation of operating systems, and the quantum increases in network bandwidth promised by asynchronous transfer mode and other emerging networking technologies, and the common workstation configuration of tomorrow will be fully capable of fulfilling both client and server roles simultaneously in ways we find it hard to imagine today.

Information Presentation

Another area that I believe we can look forward to significant and fundamental advances is in new ways to present information to the user. Exciting research is being done in graphical-user interfaces and the use of new metaphors that more closely approximate typical human cognition patterns than today's relatively simplistic desktop/icon metaphor, which is, after all, based on Xerox PARC research (now over 10 years old). New facilities using n-dimensional presentation, folding space, selective display, and heuristic learning patterns promise to revolutionize the way in which computer systems present information.

Conclusion

Client/server computing is a fundamentally different approach to developing application systems that is replacing the traditional mainframe multiuser architecture. It is no longer a question of whether it will happen in your organization. The only thing undecided is when it will happen and how far-reaching the impact will be. Those who see no need to do things differently will only be delaying the inevitable. For those who see the need and have already begun or are preparing to begin, beware. The road is still rocky, but the benefits are worth the effort.

Bibliography

Booch, G., "Objected Oriented Design", Benjamin-Cummings, 1991.

Brooks, F., "The Mythical Man Month: Essays on Software Engineering," Addison-Wesley, 1975.

Batini, C., S. Ceri, and S. Navathe, "Database Design: An Entity-Relationship Approach," Benjamin/Cummings, 1989.

Cattell, R., "Objected Data Management: Object Oriented and Extended Relational Database Systems," Addison-Wesley, 1992.

Chen, P., "Three Entity Relationship Model—Toward a Unified View of Data," *ACM Transactions on Database Systems,* vol. 1, no. 1, March 1976.

Coad, P. and E. Yourdan, "Object Oriented Analysis," Prentice-Hall Yourdan, Inc., 1990.

Codd, E., "A Relational Model for Large Shared Data Banks," *Communications of the ACM,* vol. 13, no. 6, June 1970.

Codd, E., "The Relational Model for Database Management Version 2," Addison-Wesley, 1990.

Dalziel, M. and S. Schoonover, "Changing Ways: A Practical Tool for Implementing Change within an Environment," Amacom, 1988.

Date, C., "An Introduction to Database Systems," vol. 1, Fourth Edition, Addison-Wesley, 1986.

Date, C., "An Introduction to Database Systems," vol. 2, Fourth Edition, Addison-Wesley, 1986.

DeMarco, T., "Structured Analysis and System Specification," Prentice-Hall Yourdan Inc., 1979.

DeMarco, T., "Controlling Software Projects," New York Yourdan, Inc., 1983.

Desmond, A., "Archetype and Ancestors," University of Chicago Press, 1984.

Evans, M. and J. Marciniak, "Software Quality Assurance and Management," John Wiley & Sons Inc., 1987.

Gane, G. and T. Sarson, "Structured Systems Analysis: Tools and Techniques," Improved Systems Technologies, Inc., 1977.

Moran, L. and E. Musselwhite, "Self-Directed Workteams: A Lot More than Just Teamwork," Zenger-Miller, 1988.

Orsburn, J., L. Moran, E. Musselwhite, and J. Zenger, "Self-Directed Work Teams: The New American Challenge," The Book Press, Inc., 1990.

Pearson, C., "The Hero Within: Six Archetypes We Live By," Harper and Row, 1986.

Peters, L. J., "Software Design: Methods and Techniques," New York Yourdan Inc., 1981.

Peters, T., "Thriving on Chaos," Harper and Row, 1987.

Peters, T. and N. Austin, "A Passion for Excellence," Random House, 1985.

Semprevivo, P., "Teams in Information Systems Development," New York Yourdan Inc., 1980.

Zuckerman, M. and L. Hatala, "Incredibly American: Releasing the Heart of Quality," ASQC Quality Press, 1992.

Index

Index note: An *f*. after a page number refers to a figure.

ABOUT THE AUTHOR

Larry T. Vaughn is president of Tekis, a consulting and development firm specializing in the application of client/server technologies. He was previously assistant vice president of systems development at the Frank Russell Company, and prior to that was manger of systems development and support at National Intergroup, Inc. Mr. Vaughn is a frequent contributor to industry publications and also conducts seminars on client/server issues.